Mary Berry's

Favourite

FRENCH

Recipes

MARY BERRY'S

Favourite
FRENCH
Recipes

OVER 100 EASY-TO-FOLLOW RECIPES

HAMLYN

This book was inspired by Mary Berry's *Popular French Cookery*,
first published in 1972 by Octopus Books Limited.
This new, revised and updated edition is published by Hamlyn,
an imprint of Reed Consumer Books Limited
Michelin House, 81 Fulham Road, London SW3 6RB
and Auckland, Melbourne, Singapore and Toronto.

ISBN 0 600 58553 0
A CIP catalogue record for this book is available at the British Library.
Printed in Hong Kong

ACKNOWLEDGEMENTS
Art Director Jacqui Small
Design Manager Bryan Dunn
Designer Bobby Birchall, Town Group Consultancy
Executive Editor Susan Haynes
Editor Elsa Petersen-Schepelern
Production Controller Melanie Frantz
Photographer Peter Williams
Home Economist Meg Jansz
Stylist Róisín Nield
Author Photograph Francis Loney

AUTHOR'S ACKNOWLEDGEMENT
The editor of this edition is Elsa Petersen-Schepelern, who has worked meticulously
to research the historical background to many of these recipes. She is an inveterate
traveller and has a passion for food. This has all rubbed off on the book.
MARY BERRY

CONTENTS

INTRODUCTION

THERE is a tendency to confuse French cooking with elaborate cooking. Many a sound cook has shrunk from tackling French dishes for fear that, as the recipe progresses from one complicated step to the next, she will lose her way and the final result will be a disaster.

Yet nothing could be further from the truth. Certainly there are elaborate French dishes but these are mainly confined to professional chefs and great restaurants. French home cooks have no more time to spend in the kitchen than their equivalents in other countries. Meals in a French household, therefore, tend to be simple. But simple certainly does not mean dull. Basic dishes gain a subtlety of flavour from the addition of wine, herbs or garlic, sometimes all three. French cooks make the most of the finest fresh ingredients available in season. They understand that appetites are best stimulated by appealing to three senses – sight and smell as well as taste – so that care is taken with presentation as well as with cooking.

It has been said that the French think more of their stomachs than of anything else, that they hold eating in far higher esteem than, for example, making love or making money. You don't have to spend much time in France before coming to the same conclusions. The midday meal is the highspot of the French day. Not for them an hour's lunchtime or doughy sandwich, hastily bought and absentmindedly devoured. Most French people make a bee-line for home when the morning's work is over, home to a wonderfully aromatic smell which greets them as they enter the front door, home to a colourfully laid table and a bottle of *vin ordinaire*, usually drunk from tumblers.

French cooking is not necessarily expensive. More often than not, it is the reverse. The French, by and large, are incredibly frugal. What cooks in other countries might throw away, a French cook would probably regard as the basis of the next meal. Bones go into a stockpot (why spend money on bouillon cubes?), stale bread is crisped in the oven, or oven-dried and turned into breadcrumbs, or served in soup as croûtons. Bacon rind may be fried and used as garnish, bacon fat rendered down and used. Left-over potato makes a thickening for soup.

The characteristic French knack of making something out of nothing enables them to eat well. Add to this, their superb understanding of what makes a dish, what particular ingredient in a recipe – and how much – will turn a mundane meal into a creation, and there is little wonder that French cooking is admired and imitated throughout the world. A study of French cooking shows how much reliance is put on certain ingredients, namely wine, garlic, herbs, mushrooms, oil and vinegar.

WINE

The importance of wine in cookery lies in the flavour it gives the finished dish. Some people are afraid to use wine for fear that it will make the dish alcoholic. In fact, whether the cooking is long and slow as in a casserole, or rapid as when the wine is added to a quickly-cooked dish and reduced by fast boiling to a sauce, the alcohol content is burnt out. What remains is the essence of the wine, delicate, appetizing and unmistakable.

The wine can be as cheap or as expensive as you like. You may think that the quality does not matter since it is being cooked, but a better wine adds a richness of flavour that is far superior to that of its cheaper equivalent. Sometimes, it is worthwhile sneaking a glassful of the wine that is to be served at the table. If the wine is to be drunk soon, leave red wine uncorked to reach room temperature, or re-cork white wine and put it in the refrigerator.

Unless the wine is to be drunk later, it is better to buy a half bottle than a whole one. Unused wine may be decanted into a smaller bottle, corked and stored in a the refrigerator, but do not keep it longer than two or three days. Sour wine will certainly not improve a dish. White wine, on the whole keeps better than red. You can also freeze wine in small lidded containers and use it later for cooking.

Some recipes call for fortified wines, such as Marsala, Madeira or sherry. These fortified wines, unlike ordinary ones, need not be cooked. A spoonful of sherry, for example, may be added to consommé with excellent effect.

Sometimes, spirits are used to flambé a dish. In this case the brandy, or whatever spirit is chosen, is first warmed in a soup ladle or small saucepan to ensure that it will flame, then set alight and the burning liquid poured over the meat or pancakes in the pan. The pan should be shaken gently to spread the flames. When they die down, the alcohol will have burnt away and taken with it any excess grease.

Sweet dishes may be enhanced by adding liqueur – perhaps using just a miniature bottle. This will not add a great deal to the cost of the meal, but will add enormously to its quality.

GARLIC

Garlic and the Continent seem synonymous to many people. Appreciation of the culinary virtues of garlic has remained the prerogative of the Continent and Asia. The essence of using garlic is restraint. Its flavour must never be allowed to dominate – far better to use too little than too much. In salads, for example, just rubbing round the salad bowl with a clove of garlic will give the salad a subtle lift. A little garlic in butter on French bread makes a dish in itself.

Fresh garlic is always better than any form of dried garlic, and the best way of using it is to squeeze it through a garlic press. The use of a press prevents the very persistent smell of garlic from lingering on the chopping board or on your hands. And, incidentally, the press has other uses in the kitchen. It is excellent for extracting the juice from onions or fresh herbs.

If the garlic has sprouted, peel it, and purée in a processor with 6 tablespoons olive oil to every 8 heads. Keep it in a screwtop jar in the refrigerator, and use within a month.

HERBS

Herbs, of course, are used in most forms of cooking, but often rather conservatively. The French, however, call on a wide range of herbs and use them in a great variety of ways. Country families in France grow them in their rather formal gardens, gather them and dry them in bunches suspended from the kitchen ceiling. The bunches of drying herbs make an attractive addition to kitchen décor and have the added advantage that they are always on hand. The modern commercial process of freeze-drying herbs is so quick that the herbs retain most of their colour and flavour, and the dried herbs we buy now are vastly superior to those of the past. Fresh herbs are better of course, and are now available in most supermarkets if you can't grow them yourself.

The French make excellent herb dressings for salads by steeping herbs in the dressing in a bottle for about five days. At the end of that time, the dressing is strained and re-bottled. The herbs have gone, but their delicate aroma remains.

MUSHROOMS

Mushrooms figure in so many French recipes that they are worth a study in themselves. In a French market there may be as many as eight different varieties of mushrooms on sale, each with its own subtle flavour. The mushroom of the woodlands tastes quite different from the mushroom of the fields, and the French, with typical thoroughness, are well aware of the difference each variety makes to the final dish. I feel, however, that it is much wiser to leave experimentation to the experts on edible funghi. Where mushrooms have been used in the recipes in this book, I have used the varieties commonly available, including chestnut, oyster, button and field mushrooms.

OIL

Two different kinds of oil are commonly used in France. Olive oil is used for mayonnaise and dressings, and groundnut oil, which is much cheaper, for frying. A good olive oil does not necessarily have a strong flavour. Groundnut oil (*huile d'arachide*) is almost flavourless, and some people even prefer it for salads, using herbs, seasoning, vinegar and lemon juice to sharpen the taste of the dressing or mayonnaise. Sunflower oil is an appropriate alternative.

VINEGAR

A malt vinegar salesman would have a thin time in France, except possibly from young French girls who rinse their hair in malt vinegar. In French cookery, vinegar is almost always distilled from white or red wine. Tarragon vinegar is wine vinegar flavoured with tarragon and for some dishes it is preferred to straight wine vinegar.

Cider vinegar may sometimes be substituted for the more expensive wine vinegar.

TIPS FOR KITCHEN USERS

By and large, the French are not gadget-minded and seem content to go on using equipment with which their grandmothers were happy. Really sharp knives are undoubtedly top of the list. For some reason, the French are quite expert at making really good, stainless steel and carbon steel kitchen knives. Even the cheap ones, found in any inexpensive department store in France, need no more than normal care to keep a good edge on them.

The French are also keen on graters, of varying sizes, each with a number of different blades, with which they can slice, shred or purée. Useful ideas worth copying from a French kitchen are: making French dressing in quantity, which may be bottled and stored in a cold place; making mayonnaise in quantity and storing the surplus in the refrigerator; keeping a vanilla pod in a jar of sugar, producing vanilla sugar, (useful for making custards, etc.); and keeping seasonings in a box near the cooker, handy for adjusting seasoning during cooking.

Finally, if you are shopping in France or ordering from a French menu, don't forget that the French for chicory is *endive* and the French for endive is *chicorie.*

Beginnings

The First Course

In France, these are known generally as 'hors d'oeuvres', but this term, outside France, has a specific meaning. Better, I think to call the first course 'beginnings', for this is what it is – the beginning of a meal which should leave both you and your guests feeling mellow and satisfied. The course should have two virtues – firstly, it should titillate the palate but not destroy the appetite and, secondly, it should be easy to prepare and to serve, so that you, as cook, may concentrate on the main course without worry. Most of the recipes that follow may be prepared beforehand.

1 KG/2 LB FISH, WHICH COULD
INCLUDE VARIETIES
SUCH AS:
MONKFISH, PLAICE, SOLE AND
HALIBUT

1 LARGE PINCH OF SAFFRON
THREADS

1 COOKED CRAB (OPTIONAL)

1 SMALL, SPLIT LOBSTER TAIL OR
CRAWFISH TAIL (OPTIONAL)

500 G/1 LB COOKED, WHOLE
PRAWNS WITH SHELLS

A FEW COOKED MUSSELS

4 TABLESPOONS OLIVE OIL

2 LARGE ONIONS, CHOPPED

1 SMALL HEAD OF FRESH FENNEL

1.8 LITRES/3 PINTS FISH STOCK
(SEE METHOD ON RIGHT)

4 TOMATOES, SKINNED,
DESEEDED AND CHOPPED

1 BAY LEAF

3 SPRIGS OF PARSLEY

SALT AND FRESHLY GROUND
BLACK PEPPER

6-8 SLICES OF FRENCH BREAD

Illustrated pages 10-11

PREVIOUS PAGES
Bouillabaisse (recipe this page).

BOUILLABAISSE

Ask the fishmonger to fillet and skin the fish, but keep the skin and bones for stock. Steep the saffron threads for 30 minutes in ½ cup of boiling water. Prepare the cooked crab and lobster or crawfish tail, if using. Peel the prawns, but keep the mussels in their shells. Put the skin, bones and shells from the fish and shellfish in a pan with 2.1 litres/3½ pints of water. Bring to the boil and simmer for 20 minutes, then strain off the fish stock and reserve. Discard the skin, bones and shells.

Heat the oil in a large pan, add the onions and fennel and fry slowly until softened but not coloured. Add the fresh fish, cut into chunks, to the pan and cook gently for 5 minutes. Add the saffron with its juice, the fish stock, the pre-cooked seafood and all other ingredients except the French bread. Simmer the bouillabaisse for about 3 minutes until all the fish and seafood is cooked and heated through.

Check the seasoning, discard the bay leaf and the parsley. Serve with French bread, and Aïoli if liked (see page 93).

VARIATION

Rouille: another traditional accompaniment for bouillabaisse is this hot, peppery mayonnaise, which you could serve instead of aïoli. Take 1 red pepper, cored, skinned (see page 123), deseeded and diced, and pound it in a mortar and pestle or purée it in a food processor. Add a little salt and a pinch of chilli powder. Mix together with 150 ml/¼ pint of Mayonnaise (see page 93). Serve the bouillabaisse in a big tureen, and allow your guests to help themselves, adding as much rouille as they like.

Soupe à la Du Barry

*The Comtesse du Barry was the successor to
Madame Pompadour as the mistress of the French King,
Louis XV. She has given her name to dishes which include
cauliflower, perhaps because her beautiful skin was as pale as
milk. I am sorry to tell you that Robespierre was not so
enamoured of her, and she came to a bad end
on the guillotine.*

SERVES 4-6

50 G / 2 OZ BUTTER

1 LARGE ONION, SLICED

1 FAT GARLIC CLOVE, CRUSHED

1 MEDIUM CAULIFLOWER, CUT
INTO FLORETS

1 LITRE / 1¾ PINTS CHICKEN
STOCK

4 TABLESPOONS SINGLE CREAM

SALT AND FRESHLY GROUND
BLACK PEPPER

To garnish

1 TABLESPOON CHOPPED FRESH
PARSLEY

FRIED BREAD CROÛTONS

Heat the butter in a large, heavy-based saucepan. Add the onion and garlic and fry slowly until soft. Add the cauliflower and the chicken stock, bring to the boil, cover and simmer gently for about 20 minutes.

Purée the soup in a processor or blender. Return it to the saucepan, stir in the cream and reheat the soup almost to simmering point (do not boil). Check seasoning.

Scatter parsley on top of the soup and serve with croûtons.

VARIATION

For an even creamier consistency, add about 125 g / 4 oz boiled potatoes to the cooked cauliflower before puréeing in the blender or food processor.

2 TABLESPOONS SUNFLOWER OIL

50 G / 2 OZ BUTTER

2 ONIONS, FINELY CHOPPED

125 G / 4 OZ MUSHROOMS,
FINELY CHOPPED

50 G / 2 OZ PLAIN FLOUR

1.2 LITRES / 2 PINTS BEEF STOCK

150 ML / ¼ PINT SINGLE CREAM

¼ TEASPOON GRATED NUTMEG

1 TABLESPOON CHOPPED FRESH
PARSLEY, TO GARNISH

SALT AND FRESHLY GROUND
BLACK PEPPER

MUSHROOM SOUP WITH CREAM

*It was the French in fact who, about 300 years ago,
discovered how to cultivate mushrooms 'in captivity'. Only
a few years ago, you could buy only white button mushrooms, but
now the markets and supermarkets are full of oyster mushrooms in
white or yellow, British Brown Caps, chestnut mushrooms, large,
open field mushrooms, and shiitakes. Specialist shops even
have the beautiful wild mushrooms from France. Use
ordinary white mushrooms for this recipe.*

Heat the oil in a pan, then add the butter. Add the onions and cook, until softened but not coloured. Add the mushrooms and cook for a further 3 minutes.

Sprinkle in the flour and cook for 1 minute. Gradually add the beef stock, stirring. Bring to the boil then simmer for about 5 minutes until thick and smooth.

Add the single cream, nutmeg and seasoning, and simmer for 3 minutes. Serve sprinkled with parsley.

VARIATION

If you would like to give an extra blast of 'mushroomy-ness' to this recipe, soak a tablespoon of dried cèpes or porcini in a little boiling water for about 30 minutes, then add the strained water and the mushrooms to the recipe.

Tomato and Marjoram Soup

Sweet marjoram is the more elegant, delicate Northern cousin of the vigorous wild oregano of Greece and other parts of Southern Europe. It is excellent with meat and fish, and gives a sweet, slightly spicy lift to soups.

SERVES 4

25G/1 OZ BUTTER

1 ONION, SLICED

25 G/1 OZ PLAIN FLOUR

900 ML/1½ PINTS CHICKEN STOCK

½ TEASPOON GROUND NUTMEG

1 TEASPOON CASTER SUGAR

1 TEASPOON PAPRIKA

1 TEASPOON CHOPPED FRESH MARJORAM

1 BAY LEAF

2-3 SPRIGS OF FLAT LEAF PARSLEY

500 G/1 LB RIPE TOMATOES, QUARTERED

SALT AND FRESHLY GROUND BLACK PEPPER

Melt the butter, add the onion and fry slowly until softened but not coloured, then sprinkle in the flour, add the chicken stock and bring to the boil, stirring. Add the rest of the ingredients except the seasoning.

Simmer, covered, for 30 minutes until soft. Remove the bay leaf, purée the soup in a blender or food processor, then sieve to remove the skin. Bring back to the boil and check the seasoning before serving with good, crusty French bread.

VARIATIONS

Tomato and Basil Soup: tomato and basil seem to have a special affinity for each other. For a delicious variation to the main recipe, omit the paprika, nutmeg, marjoram and parsley, and substitute 1 tablespoon chopped basil. Garnish with sprigs of basil before serving.

Tomato and Chive Soup: peel and deseed 500 g/1 lb ripe tomatoes, and purée them in a blender or food processor with 900 ml/1½ pints chicken stock, a teaspoon of sugar, salt and freshly ground black pepper. Place in a saucepan and bring quickly to boiling point. Take off the heat immediately, and serve, with a tablespoon of snipped chives sprinkled over each serving. You could also swirl in a tablespoon of crème fraîche.

1.5 KG/3 LB PUMPKIN
OR 750 G/1½ LB EACH OF
PUMPKIN AND POTATO

600 ML/1 PINT CHICKEN STOCK

3 TABLESPOONS FLOUR

300 ML/½ PINT HOT MILK

BEURRE MANIÉ, MADE WITH
40 G/11/2 OZ FLOUR MIXED
WITH 40 G/11/2 OZ BUTTER
(SEE PAGE 122)

125 ML/4 FL OZ DOUBLE CREAM
OR CRÈME FRAÎCHE

A PINCH OF NUTMEG

SALT AND FRESHLY GROUND
BLACK PEPPER

SPRIGS OF CHERVIL,
TO GARNISH

PUMPKIN SOUP

*Pumpkin is not as widely used in Britain as it should be.
It is sweet and delicious, and splendid in soups, purées and gratins.
Try this pumpkin soup made with pumpkin, or half-and-half with
potato – and don't forget the nutmeg; nutmeg and pumpkin is
one of those 'marriages made in heaven'.*

Cut the pumpkin into large slices and peel. Remove and discard the seeds and the fibrous section around them. Cut the pieces into large chunks, about the same size as for boiling potatoes. Peel and cut up the potatoes, if using.

Place the pumpkin in a saucepan with just enough water to cover. Add salt, bring to the boil and cook until just tender. Purée in a blender or food processor, then return to the saucepan. Add the chicken stock, stir, and bring to the boil, then stir in the hot milk. To thicken the soup, pinch off pieces of the *beurre manié* and whisk them into the soup. Serve hot, with a swirl of double cream or crème fraîche, a sprinkle of nutmeg and a few sprigs of fresh chervil, to garnish.

VARIATIONS

Pumpkin Soup with Onion: finely chop 1 large onion and fry in 90 g (3 oz) butter until softened but not browned. Then add the pumpkin and proceed as in the main recipe.

Pumpkin Soup with Beans: French peasant soups sometimes include beans such as cannellini beans (add 250 g/8 oz of cooked cannellini beans to the main recipe), 1 or 2 cloves of crushed garlic and cooked, shredded ham (about 125 g/4 oz).

Pumpkin Purée: a thicker pumpkin purée makes an excellent sauce for dishes such as risotto.

French Onion Soup

SERVES 4

2 LARGE ONIONS, SLICED

35 G/1½ OZ BUTTER

1 TEASPOON CASTER SUGAR

35 G/1½ OZ PLAIN FLOUR

1.2 LITRES/2 PINTS BEEF STOCK

4 SLICES FRENCH BREAD

50 G/2 OZ GRATED GRUYÈRE CHEESE

SALT AND FRESHLY GROUND BLACK PEPPER

Traditionally, the bread is put on top of the soup, with cheese sprinkled on top, and then grilled. However, it is easy to crack the dish this way, so I suggest you do this separately. Adding sugar to the onions helps them to caramelize.

Brown the onions slowly in the butter. Add the sugar and cook for a few minutes until rich golden brown. Add the flour and cook for 1 minute. Add the beef stock and bring to the boil, stirring. Simmer for about 15 minutes until tender, then add salt and pepper to taste.

Toast onc side of the bread, then sprinkle the grated cheese on the untoasted side. Grill until the cheese has melted. Put one slice of the grilled toast in each soup bowl and pour the soup over the top.

Fresh Herb Pâté

SERVES 4 AS A STARTER

175 G/6 OZ RICH CREAM CHEESE

150 ML/½ PINT DOUBLE CREAM,

1 TEASPOON CHOPPED FRESH THYME LEAVES

1 TABLESPOON CHOPPED FRESH DILL

1 TABLESPOON CHOPPED FRESH CHIVES

2 FAT CLOVES OF GARLIC, CRUSHED

SALT AND FRESHLY GROUND BLACK PEPPER

Make this the day before it is needed so that the flavours blend well. Serve on vine leaves or blackcurrant leaves; as part of a cheese board; or in a pâté dish; or spread on biscuits and topped with fresh herbs, to serve with drinks.

Blend the cheese and cream in a processor. Mix in the herbs and seasoning. Turn into a 450 ml/¾ pint dish and chill before serving. Serve with crisp biscuits or crusty French bread.

2 SMOKED MACKEREL FILLETS

75 G/3 OZ CREAM CHEESE

JUICE OF ½ LEMON

300 G/10 OZ BUTTER, MELTED

SALT AND FRESHLY GROUND
BLACK PEPPER

CHOPPED FRESH FLAT LEAF
PARSLEY, TO GARNISH

PÂTÉ OF SMOKED MACKEREL

Smoked mackerel can be bought at large fishmongers, supermarkets and delicatessens. This pâté keeps well in a home freezer, and any extra makes a very good sandwich filling,

Purée the mackerel in a food processor or blender. Gradually add the remaining ingredients and mix until smooth or, if making by hand, mash the mackerel with the cream cheese and then add the other ingredients. Check seasoning.

Turn into 6 small ramekins and chill before serving. Serve with hot toast and sprinkled with chopped flat leaf parsley.

VARIATION

Pâté of Smoked Trout: the above recipe is also very good made with smoked trout. Spoon the mixture into small ramekins, lined with clingfilm, folding the ends over the pâté to keep the air out. Chill.

When ready to serve, pull the ends gently to ease the pâté out of the ramekins.

Make a salad of mixed salad leaves, such as rocket, lambs' lettuce and frisée, with a French Dressing made with light olive oil mixed with walnut oil (see page 91). Place a little salad on to 6 entrée plates, and place the pâtés beside the leaves.

BRANDADE OF KIPPER

A smooth, smoked fish pâté, based on the traditional Provençal dish, Brandade de Morue, which is a purée of salt cod. Kippers are easier to handle and easier to find in Britain – and I think they taste even better than the original.

SERVES 6

4 LARGE KIPPER FILLETS

40 G / 1½ OZ BUTTER

JUICE OF ½ LARGE LEMON

300 ML / ½ PINT DOUBLE CREAM

SALT AND FRESHLY GROUND
BLACK PEPPER

Dot the kippers with butter and grill for about 10 minutes until the flesh easily comes away from the skin. Skin the fish and purée the kippers with their juices, lemon juice, and cream in a blender or food processor, or mash with a fork until smooth.

Taste and adjust the seasoning. Spoon into 6 individual small ramekins and chill for 1 hour until set. Serve the with hot toast and butter.

VARIATION

My favourite accompaniment for pâtés and cheeses is good French bread. For a special occasion, you may like to try Melba Toast, named after the great 19th Century soprano, who was, like many opera singers, waging a constant battle with her waistline. Considering the number of famous French dishes named after her, it was no wonder!

Melba Toast: is a delicious accompaniment to this and other pâtés in this book. Lightly toast slices of bread and, while still hot, cut off the crusts. Using a very sharp knife, slice through each piece of toast horizontally, to produce two very thin slices of toast. Brown for a few moments in a preheated oven at 200°C (400°F) Gas Mark 6 until crisp and golden. Store in an air-tight tin until ready to use.

1 SLICE OF BROWN BREAD

250 G/8 OZ PIGS' LIVER

375 G/12 OZ SMOKED COOKED
BACON, CUBED

1 TABLESPOON CLEAR HONEY

2 TEASPOONS SOFT BROWN
SUGAR

125 G/4 OZ PORK SAUSAGEMEAT

3 FAT GARLIC CLOVES, CRUSHED

GRATED RIND OF ½ LEMON

1 ONION, CHOPPED

2 TEASPOONS CHOPPED FRESH
THYME LEAVES

¼ TEASPOON GROUND
ALLSPICE

¼ TEASPOON GROUND NUTMEG

1 EGG

1-2 TABLESPOONS DRY SHERRY

SALT AND FRESHLY GROUND
BLACK PEPPER

*To garnish
(optional)*

1 LARGE LEMON, SLICED, OR
5 RASHERS BACON

PÂTÉ MAISON

Buy a small bacon joint – a hock would be ideal – cook it slowly in unsalted water until tender, then strip all the meat off the bone.

Process the bread and the liver in a food processor until smooth. Add the cubed bacon, honey, sugar, sausagemeat, garlic, grated lemon rind, chopped onion, thyme, spices, egg, sherry and seasoning. Process until the ingredients are mixed but still chunky.

Slice the lemon very thinly and use to line the base of a greased 1.2 litre/2 pint round or oval ovenproof casserole (if preferred, line the base and sides with rashers of bacon instead). Fill with the pâté, cover with a lid or foil, and place in a *bain-marie*, half filled with hot water (see page 123). Cook in a preheated oven at 160°C (325°F) Gas Mark 3 for 2 hours, or until the juices run clear when the pâté is pierced with a knife.

Allow to cool completely before turning out and serving. This pâté is even better the day after it's made.

VARIATIONS

Chicken Liver Pâté: substitute 250 g/8 oz chicken livers for the pork liver in the above recipe. Frozen chicken livers, readily available in supermarkets, are very reasonable.

Lambs' Liver Pâtè: although it is not at all authentic, you may enjoy the milder taste of lambs' liver.

EGGS EN COCOTTE WITH AUBERGINES

Aubergines first arrived in Europe from India in the 13th Century, arriving in France by the 17th Century. Now they are used in many recipes from the South of France, especially from Provence, and in company with tomatoes and onions, as here. They can be bitter, and must be blanched, or cut and salted before using, in order to remove their slightly bitter dark juices. Dry the slices of aubergine thoroughly before cooking.

Cut the aubergines in 1 cm/½ inch dice, put on a plate and sprinkle thickly with salt. Leave for 15-30 minutes minutes, then rinse in cold water and dry on kitchen paper.

Heat the oil in a pan, add the aubergines and onion, cover and cook gently for 20 minutes. Add the tomatoes and cook for a further 10 minutes without the lid.

Remove the pan from the heat, check the seasoning and place in a large, shallow ovenproof dish. Break the eggs into the dish and spoon over the cream.

Place the dishes in a baking tray and cook in a preheated oven at 180°C (350°F) Gas Mark 4 for about 10 minutes or until the eggs are just set.

SERVES 6

250 G/8 OZ AUBERGINES

4 TABLESPOONS OLIVE OIL

1 LARGE ONION, SLICED

3 TOMATOES, SKINNED AND SLICED

6 EGGS

6 TABLESPOONS SINGLE CREAM

SALT AND FRESHLY GROUND BLACK PEPPER

SERVES 6

100 G/4 OZ LEAF SPINACH

300 ML/½ PINT MILK

40 G/1½ OZ BUTTER

40 G/1½ OZ PLAIN FLOUR

¼ TEASPOON GRATED NUTMEG

50 G/2 OZ GRATED GRUYÈRE
CHEESE

3 EGGS, SEPARATED

50 G/2 OZ GRATED PARMESAN
CHEESE

300 ML/½ PINT DOUBLE CREAM,
SEASONED

Illustrated opposite

TWICE-COOKED CHEESE SOUFFLÉS

You can cook the soufflés ahead – assemble them in the gratin dish without adding the cream, cover and keep in the refrigerator for up to 24 hours. Pour over the cream and the rest of the Parmesan just before the second stage. Delicious for lunch, or as a first course at dinner.

Wash the spinach and shred finely. Bring to the boil in the milk, stir, and set aside. Melt the butter in a large pan, remove from the heat and blend in the flour. Return to the heat and cook for 1 minute, stirring. Add the spinach and milk a little at a time and bring to the boil stirring constantly. Simmer until the sauce is thick and smooth. Remove the pan from the heat and beat in the salt, pepper, nutmeg and Gruyère. When these are well incorporated, stir in the egg yolks. Whisk the egg whites until stiff and fold into the sauce mixture.

Butter 6 small ramekins very generously and spoon in the mixture. Place them in a small roasting tin, pour boiling water into the tin until half way up the dishes. Cook in a preheated oven at 220°C (425°F) Gas Mark 7 for 15-20 minutes or until the soufflés are golden, firm and springy to the touch. After 12 minutes, turn around if necessary to brown evenly. Leave for 5-10 minutes to shrink back in the soufflé dish.

Butter a shallow gratin dish (large enough to hold the soufflés without touching). Sprinkle with half the Parmesan.

Run the blade of a small palette knife around the edges of the soufflés then unmould them into the gratin dish. Pour over the cream, sprinkle with the remaining Parmesan and bake for another 15-20 minutes or until bubbling and brown.

SERVES 4

75 G/3 OZ BUTTER

50 G/2 OZ PLAIN FLOUR

300 ML/½ PINT MILK

75 G/3 OZ GRUYÈRE CHEESE,
GRATED

25 G/1 OZ PARMESAN CHEESE,
GRATED

2 TEASPOONS DIJON MUSTARD

3 LARGE EGGS, SEPARATED

SALT AND FRESHLY GROUND
BLACK PEPPER

CLASSIC CHEESE SOUFFLÉ

Many people are nervous of making soufflés. But it isn't difficult – even if you plan to serve one at a dinner party. You prepare the mixture as far as adding the yolks and cheese, and then refrigerate and forget about it until about fifty minutes or so before serving. Then, you whisk the egg whites until stiff and fold them into the prepared mixture. Pour into the soufflé dish and place in the oven. Ask your guests to sit down, fill their wine glasses, and by the time the soufflé arrives, they should all be firm friends!

Butter a 1.2 litre/2 pint soufflé dish. Melt the butter in a pan. Stir in the flour, and then blend in the milk. Bring to the boil, stirring constantly. Simmer for 3 minutes. Remove the pan from the heat and beat in the Gruyère and Parmesan, mustard and seasoning. Beat in the egg yolks, one at a time.

Whisk the egg whites until stiff, then fold into the cheese mixture. Turn into the prepared dish and cook in a preheated oven at 190°C (375°F) Gas Mark 5 for about 45 minutes, until the soufflé is well risen and the top is set and slightly crusty. Serve at once, with a watercress salad.

VARIATIONS

Smoked Salmon Soufflé: add 75 g/3 oz of smoked salmon pieces to the recipe above, and serve the soufflé with a salad of mixed green leaves.

Ham Soufflé: chop 150 g/5 oz finely chopped lean ham. Add to the Cheese Soufflé mixture.

EGGS MORNAY

SERVES 4

4 EGGS

25 G/1 OZ BUTTER

25 G/1 OZ PLAIN FLOUR

150 ML/¼ PINT MILK

50 G/2 OZ GRUYÈRE CHEESE,
GRATED

25 G/1 OZ PARMESAN CHEESE,
GRATED

1 TEASPOON MADE MUSTARD

SALT AND FRESHLY GROUND
BLACK PEPPER

Boil the eggs for only 8 minutes so they are not completely hard, then cool under cold running water. Carefully peel the shells from the eggs.

Melt the butter in a pan, add the flour and cook for 1 minute. Stir in the milk and bring to boiling point, stirring constantly. Simmer for 2 minutes, remove the pan from the heat and stir in most of the cheese. Add mustard and plenty of seasoning, cut the eggs in half lengthways and arrange in an ovenproof serving dish. Spoon over the sauce, sprinkle with the remaining cheese, brown under the preheated grill and serve with a green salad and toast.

VARIATION

Poached Eggs Mornay: fry 8 slices of good French bread in a little butter. Place 2 slices in each of 4 shallow ramekins and top with 2 poached eggs. Pour over the Mornay Sauce as in the main recipe, sprinkle with the grated cheese, brown under a preheated grill, and serve.

Note: for perfectly-shaped poached eggs – place the unshelled eggs in a bowl and cover with hot (not quite boiling) water for exactly 1 minute, to set the white a little. Then crack the eggs into a cup, slip them into boiling water, reduce the heat, and simmer until the eggs are cooked.

FRENCH OMELETTE

*The size of the pan is very important for an omelette.
Use a 15 cm/6 inch pan for two eggs and a 18 cm/7 inch
pan for a three egg quantity.*

Beat the eggs with a fork until lightly mixed, then beat in the seasoning. Slowly heat a heavy 18 cm/7 inch diameter omelette pan until very hot. Add the butter, and as soon as it has melted, pour in the eggs. Using the fork, keep drawing some of the mixture to the middle from the sides of the pan. Cook for 1½–2 minutes until soft but not runny. Remove the pan from the heat and, using the fork, fold the omelette away from you, but only half over. Tilt the pan over a hot plate. The omelette will slip forward on to the plate, neatly folded.

VARIATIONS

Cheese: sprinkle 50 g/2 oz finely grated cheese over the egg mixture after it has been added to the pan.

Fines Herbes: add 1 tablespoon chopped, mixed fresh herbs, to the eggs before cooking.

Onion: fry 1 large onion in butter, then cool, and add to the egg mixture before pouring into the omelette pan.

Kidney: peel, core and chop 2 lambs' kidneys, fry with a little onion and pile into the cooked omelette.

Mushroom: fry 50 g/2 oz chopped mushrooms in butter and fold into the cooked omelette.

Shellfish: roughly chop a handful of cooked prawns, or a few tablespoons of cooked crab meat. Toss in a little butter in a separate frying pan until warmed through, and pile into the omelette when it is about half-cooked.

Little Quiches with Prawns and Chives

These small tarts make a substantial beginning to a summer dinner party.

For the pastry
SHORTCRUST PASTRY MADE WITH 175 G/6 OZ PLAIN FLOUR, 75 G/3 OZ BUTTER AND 2 TABLESPOONS COLD WATER (SEE RECIPE BELOW)

For the filling
175 G/6 OZ SHELLED, COOKED PRAWNS, ROUGHLY CHOPPED

1 TABLESPOON CHOPPED FRESH CHIVES

1 EGG

150 G/5 OZ SINGLE CREAM

25 G/1 OZ MATURE CHEDDAR CHEESE, FINELY GRATED

SALT AND FRESHLY GROUND BLACK PEPPER

Use the pastry to line 12 individual patty tins. Bake 'blind' (see page 122) in a preheated oven at 200°C (400°F) Gas Mark 6 for 7 minutes. Remove the paper and baking beans or foil.

Divide the prawns between the pastry cases and sprinkle with chives. Blend together the remaining ingredients except the cheese, and spoon into the cases. Sprinkle with cheese and bake at 180°C (350°F) Gas Mark 4 for about 20 minutes or until the filling is pale golden and lightly set.

VARIATIONS

Smoked Fish and Chives: substitute 175 g/6 oz flaked, cooked, smoked fish for the prawns, then sprinkle with chives.
Bacon and Chives: instead of the prawns, substitute 175 g/6 oz bacon, diced and fried until crisp, then sprinkle with chives.

Shortcrust Pastry

MAKES 250 G/8 OZ PASTRY (SEE COOK'S NOTES, PAGE 123)

250 G/8 OZ PLAIN FLOUR
125 G/4 OZ BUTTER

3 TABLESPOONS COLD WATER

SALT

Measure the flour and salt into a bowl. Cut the butter into small pieces, then rub into the flour with the tips of the fingers until the mixture resembles fine breadcrumbs. Add enough water to mix to a firm dough. Wrap in clingfilm and allow to rest in the refrigerator for at least 30 minutes. When ready to cook, roll out thinly on a floured table and use as required.

SHORTCRUST PASTRY, MADE WITH
125 G/4 OZ FLOUR,
2 OZ BUTTER AND
1 TABLESPOON COLD WATER
(SEE PAGE 27)

For the filling

1 MEDIUM ONION, CHOPPED

25 G/1 OZ BUTTER

125 G/4 OZ RINDLESS STREAKY
BACON

1 EGG

150 ML/¼ PINT SINGLE CREAM

50 G/2 OZ GRATED GRUYÈRE
CHEESE

SALT AND FRESHLY GROUND
BLACK PEPPER

QUICHE LORRAINE

Use the pastry to line an 18 cm/7 inch fluted flan ring placed on a baking tray. Chill in the refrigerator for 10 minutes then bake 'blind' (see page 122), in a preheated oven at 220°C (425°F) Gas Mark 7 for 15 minutes. Remove from the oven and discard the paper and baking beans or foil.

Fry the onion in the butter until softened but not coloured. Chop the bacon and add to the pan. Fry the onion and bacon together until golden brown. Blend together the egg, cream and seasoning. Place the onion and bacon in the flan case. Pour the egg mixture on top and sprinkle with the grated cheese. Cook in a preheated oven at 180°C (350°F) Gas Mark 4 for 35 minutes or until the filling is set.

VARIATIONS

Smoked Salmon Quiche: omit the bacon and add 50 g/2 oz finely chopped smoked salmon pieces. There is no need to fry them first, and it is important not to add too much salt to this mixture, since the salmon is already salty.

Spinach and Ham Quiche: omit the bacon and add 125 g/4 oz chopped cooked ham and 125 g/4 oz chopped leaf spinach which has been tossed in a little butter over a high heat for about 1 minute before adding.

RED PEPPERS WITH GRUYÈRE AND BACON

I prefer to use red peppers in this recipe, though yellow or orange ones will do just as well. I have even seen purple ones in the markets.

Sprinkle the aubergine with salt and leave for 15 minutes, then rinse and pat dry on kitchen paper.

Heat the oil in a pan, add the aubergine and onion. Cover and fry gently until softened, for about 5 minutes. Stir in the flour, then add the remaining ingredients for the filling and bring to boiling point. Check seasonings.

Place the peppers close together in a shallow ovenproof dish. Fill with the mixture and cover with foil. Cook in a preheated oven at 200°C (400°F) Gas Mark 6 for 20 minutes until the peppers are soft. Lift off the foil, sprinkle with cheese and return to the oven for about 10 minutes to brown the top.

SERVES 4

4 MEDIUM RED PEPPERS, CORED, DESEEDED AND HALVED LENGTHWAYS

For the filling

1 SMALL AUBERGINE, CUT INTO 1 CM/½ INCH DICE

3 TABLESPOONS OLIVE OIL

1 LARGE ONION, CHOPPED

25 G/1 OZ PLAIN FLOUR

375 G/12 OZ COOKED HAM OR BACON PIECES, CUBED

1 TEASPOON CHOPPED FRESH OREGANO

300 ML/½ PINT CHICKEN STOCK

2 TABLESPOONS TOMATO PURÉE

75 G/3 OZ GRUYÈRE CHEESE, GRATED

SALT AND FRESHLY GROUND BLACK PEPPER

PIPERADE

This is a dish from the Basque country – very homely, and good for the sort of Sunday breakfast which is almost lunch.

Fry the onion in the oil until softened but not coloured. Add the garlic and cook for 1-2 minutes more. Add the peppers, tomatoes, thyme or marjoram and salt and pepper to taste.

Cook until the tomatoes have reduced down, and most of the liquid evaporated, then stir the eggs into the mixture. They will begin to look like creamy scrambled eggs.

Serve with crispy bacon or slices of the traditional Bayonne ham, and lots of French bread to mop up the delicious juices.

SERVES 4

1 LARGE ONION, CHOPPED

1 TABLESPOON OLIVE OIL

3 CLOVES OF GARLIC, CRUSHED

4 RED OR YELLOW PEPPERS, CORED, DESEEDED, SKINNED AND SLICED (SEE PAGE 123)

1 KG/2 LB RIPE RED TOMATOES, SKINNED, DESEEDED AND QUARTERED

1 TABLESPOON CHOPPED FRESH THYME OR MARJORAM LEAVES

4 EGGS, BEATEN

SALT AND FRESHLY GROUND BLACK PEPPER

For the poppy seed base

50 G/2 OZ POPPY SEEDS

175 G/6 OZ PLAIN FLOUR

1 TABLESPOON LIGHT
MUSCOVADO SUGAR

90 G/3 ½ OZ BUTTER, CUBED

ABOUT 1-2 TABLESPOONS WATER

SALT AND FRESHLY GROUND
BLACK PEPPER

For the topping

1 TABLESPOON OLIVE OIL

25G/1 OZ BUTTER

500 G/½ LB LARGE, MILD
ONIONS, FINELY SLICED

3 FAT CLOVES OF GARLIC,
CRUSHED

250 G/8 OZ FIRM RIPE
TOMATOES, SKINNED AND
DESEEDED

6 LEAVES BASIL, TORN INTO
SMALL PIECES

1 TEASPOON SUGAR

SALT AND FRESHLY GROUND
BLACK PEPPER

To assemble

16 ANCHOVY FILLETS

16 PITTED BLACK OLIVES

FRESH BASIL OR CHOPPED,
FRESH, FLAT LEAF PARSLEY,
TO GARNISH

Illustrated opposite

PISSALADIÈRE

To make the poppy seed base

Place the poppy seeds, flour, sugar, butter, salt and pepper in the processor. Blend until it resembles fine breadcrumbs, then add the water. Process until just beginning to gather together into a ball, adding a little more liquid if necessary.

Roll out straight on to a flat baking sheet into a circle about 30 cm/12 inches in diameter. Pinch up the edge all round. The pastry is quite crumbly but patches up easily and you can help to make the circle using your hands as well as a rolling pin. Rest in the fridge while you make the topping.

To make the topping

Heat the oil and butter in a frying pan, add the onions and garlic, and fry gently until golden, stirring all the time. Add the tomatoes, basil, sugar, salt and pepper, and cook uncovered until the mixture thickens.

To assemble

Spread the filling over the poppy seed base, add the anchovy fillets, arranging in the form of a star or lattice, and press the olives lightly into the top. Bake in a preheated oven at 220°C (425°F) Gas Mark 7 for 30 minutes or until the pastry is crisp. Scatter with torn fresh basil or chopped parsley and serve hot.

500 G/1 LB FIRM TOMATOES,
SKINNED

APPROXIMATELY 750 G/1½ LB
CANNED ARTICHOKE HEARTS,
DRAINED

SALT AND FRESHLY GROUND
BLACK PEPPER

1 TABLESPOON CHOPPED, FRESH
PARSLEY

For the dressing

1 TEASPOON CASTER SUGAR

1 TABLESPOON CHOPPED FRESH
CHIVES

5 TABLESPOONS OLIVE OIL

2 TABLESPOONS WINE VINEGAR

1 TEASPOON CHOPPED FRESH
BASIL

PER SERVING

1 LARGE GLOBE ARTICHOKE
PER PERSON

1 LEMON, HALVED

SALT

Suggested accompaniments
MELTED BUTTER,
HOLLANDAISE (PAGE 92),
MAYONNAISE (PAGE 93),
FRENCH DRESSING (PAGE 91),
SOURED CREAM BLENDED
WITH FRENCH DRESSING AND
LOTS OF MUSTARD.

ARTICHOKE HEARTS WITH TOMATO AND CHIVE DRESSING

Blend all the dressing ingredients together and set aside.

Slice the tomatoes thinly, and arrange on small individual plates. Arrange the artichoke hearts on top and spoon over the dressing. Leave in a cold place until just before serving. Scatter with parsley and serve with brown bread and butter.

FRESH GLOBE ARTICHOKES

The globe artichoke, a relative of the thistle, is an attractive, leafy vegetable. Choose large fresh green ones and store them in a polythene bag in the refrigerator for up to a week. The French ones, available in mid to late summer, are the largest and best.

Cut off the stalks from the artichokes, and cut off the top of the globe and the prickly top of each leaf. Rub each cut with half a lemon to stop discoloration. Place the artichokes in a saucepan, cover with boiling water and cook until tender – about 40 minutes, or until you can easily pull out a leaf. Drain them upside down, and serve hot or cold.

To eat, pull off each leaf, one by one, and dip the fleshy end into one of the suggested accompaniments. Then, with the teeth, scrape off the fleshy part and enjoy it. Discard the leaves when they have all been removed, then with a knife and fork take out the 'choke' (the hairy bit) and you are left with the fond, or fleshy base. This is the best part, and you eat it with a knife and fork and more of the chosen sauce.

WILD MUSHROOMS OR CHAMPIGNONS ON TOAST

There are just a few shops in Britain where you can find those beautiful wild mushrooms you see in markets all over France – chanterelles, cèpes, morels, girolles, to name just a few. If you are lucky enough to find them, you should treat them as the highlight of a meal. Even with ordinary mushrooms, this is a delicious way to serve them, and if you add just a few dried cèpes (often sold as porcini), it will give just a hint of 'the real thing'.

To make the toast

Fry the garlic gently in the butter and oil. Fry the bread gently on both sides until brown. Remove. Place one slice of browned bread on each plate and set aside in a warm place.

To make the mushrooms

Melt the butter with 1 tablespoon oil and the garlic. Add the mushrooms, and sauté them gently until done. Toward the end of the cooking time, add the reserved juice (if using dried mushroms) and sprinkle with chopped parsley. Check the seasoning, then spoon the mushrooms and their buttery juices over the slices of browned bread. Serve very hot.

VARIATION

For a more spectacular presentation, serve in croustades of bread. Remove the crusts from some good stale bread and cut into slices about 6 cm/2½ inches thick. Deep-fry in hot oil, then cut a hole in one side and remove the bread from inside. You should have a 'box' of brown crispy toast. Fill with sautéed mushrooms and serve with a sauce made from reduced beef stock. Garnish with a few green salad leaves, and serve.

SERVES 6

For the toast

1 GARLIC CLOVE, CRUSHED

1 TABLESPOON BUTTER

1 TABLESPOON OLIVE OIL

4 THICK SLICES OF GOOD BREAD

For the mushrooms

3 TABLESPOONS BUTTER

1 TABLESPOON OLIVE OIL

2 CLOVES GARLIC, CRUSHED

1 KG/2 LB WILD MUSHROOMS
OR
1 KG/2 LB MIXED CULTIVATED MUSHROOMS,
PLUS
25 G/1 OZ OF DRIED CÈPES OR PORCINI, STEEPED IN 1 CUP OF BOILING WATER FOR 1 HOUR, THEN STRAINED AND THE JUICE RESERVED

SALT AND FRESHLY GROUND BLACK PEPPER

1 TABLESPOON CHOPPED FRESH FLAT LEAF PARSLEY

SERVES 4

1.5 KG/3 LB FRESH MUSSELS

25 G/1 OZ BUTTER

4 SMALL ONIONS, CHOPPED

8 PARSLEY STALKS

2 SPRIGS FRESH THYME

1 BAY LEAF

300 ML/½ PINT DRY WHITE WINE

A LITTLE SALT, TO TASTE, AND
FRESHLY GROUND BLACK PEPPER

1 BUNCH CHOPPED FRESH
FLAT LEAF PARSLEY

For the beurre manié
(see page 123)

25 G/1 OZ BUTTER, BLENDED
WITH
25 G/1 OZ PLAIN FLOUR

Illustrated opposite

MOULES MARINIÈRE

When buying mussels, allow 500 g/1 lb per person.
Take care not to overcook them. They only take a few minutes, just
until the shells open.

Scrape and clean each mussel with a strong knife, removing every trace of seaweed, mud and beard. Wash well and discard any mussels which do not close tightly when tapped sharply against the work surface.

Melt the butter in a large pan, add the onions and fry until softened but not coloured. Add the herbs, pepper and wine and then the mussels. Cover with a tightly fitting lid and cook quickly, shaking the pan constantly, until the mussels open – about 5-6 minutes. Lift the mussels out of the pan, and keep hot in a covered serving dish. Discard any mussels which have not opened.

Reduce the cooking liquid to about 300 ml/½ pint. Remove the sprigs of thyme, parsley stalks and bay leaf. Drop the *beurre-manié* into the simmering stock a teaspoon at a time and whisk until the stock is smooth and thickened (see page 123). Taste and adjust the seasoning.

Pour the sauce over the mussels and scatter with plenty of chopped parsley. Serve with crusty French bread and butter or Garlic Herb Bread (see page 37).

Finger bowls are a help, as picking up mussels is a messy process. One idea is to use a pair of empty shells as tweezers to extract the meat from the mussels. You will also need a dish for the discarded shells.

SERVES 6

For the sauce

50 G/2 OZ BUTTON
MUSHROOMS, SLICED

75 ML/3 FL OZ VERMOUTH OR
DRY WHITE WINE

300 ML/½ PINT DOUBLE CREAM

1 TEASPOON CHOPPED FRESH
DILL

SALT AND FRESHLY GROUND
BLACK PEPPER

For the parcels

6 SHEETS FILO PASTRY,
TO PRODUCE 12 PIECES
15 CM/6 INCHES SQUARE

MELTED BUTTER AND OIL,
TO BRUSH

350 G/12 OZ SALMON FILLET,
SKINNED AND CUT INTO
THIN STRIPS

SALMON FILO PARCELS

The parcels and sauce can be made the day before, and then cooked just before serving. Packets of filo – strudel pastry – can be found in any good supermarket.

First make the sauce. Cook the mushrooms in the wine, then remove from the liquid and reduce it to about 3 tablespoons. Add the cream. Simmer until the sauce reaches a light coating consistency. Remove from the heat and season to taste. Add the dill. Transfer one-third of the sauce to a small bowl and allow to cool. Keep the remainder to reheat later.

Lift out 6 sheets of pastry and cover with a damp tea towel. Take 3 sheets and place flat on a work surface. Brush with a mixture of melted butter and oil and cut each in half. Place one-sixth of the strips of salmon and the cooled mushroom mixture into the centre of the square of filo, and top with a teaspoon of sauce from the bowl. Bundle into a parcel. Brush the 3 remaining squares with butter, cut each in half, and place a bundle in the centre of each square. Draw up to the neck. Lift the 6 little parcels on to a greased baking sheet. Brush each with more melted butter and oil. Cook immediately and serve, or keep covered in the refrigerator until required.

Cook in a preheated oven at 220°C (425°F) Gas Mark 7 for about 15 minutes until pale golden and crisp. Turn once. Serve as soon as possible with the remaining cream sauce, reheated but not boiled.

VARIATION

Prawn or Scallop Filo Parcels: substitute 350 g/12 oz sliced scallops or peeled, chopped prawns for the salmon fillet.

GARLIC HERB BREAD

Cut the loaf in 2.5 cm/1 inch slices. Blend together the remaining ingredients and spread the mixture between the slices of bread and reassemble the loaf.

Wrap the loaf in foil and cook in a preheated oven at 220°C (425°F) Gas Mark 7 for about 15-20 minutes. Serve hot, divided in slices.

SERVES 6

1 FRENCH LOAF

ABOUT 75 G/3 OZ BUTTER

3 FAT GARLIC CLOVES, CRUSHED

2 TABLESPOONS CHOPPED FRESH
LEAFY HERBS, SUCH AS PARSLEY,
CHIVES AND WATERCRESS OR
LAND CRESS

CRUDITÉS

*A delicious, fresh starter to an informal summer lunch –
and also good to serve at a drinks party. It consists of a selection of
prepared, raw vegetables served with Aïoli (see page 93), a
garlic flavoured mayonnaise. Use vegetables in season,
for example, those listed on the right.*

Place 1 quantity of aïoli in the centre of a large serving platter. Surround it with a selection of raw, fresh vegetables, cut into bite-sized pieces, which guests should eat with their fingers, dipping each piece into the aïoli.

A selection of fresh vegetables in season, which could include the following:

FENNEL,
CUT INTO PIECES

CAULIFLOWER,
BROKEN INTO SMALL FLORETS

CUCUMBER,
CUT INTO 5 CM/2 INCH STRIPS

WHOLE RADISHES

MANGETOUT

YOUNG BEANS

CARROTS,
CUT IN STRIPS

CELERY,
CUT INTO 5 CM/2 INCH
LENGTHS

CHICORY,
DIVIDED INTO LEAVES

RED OR YELLOW PEPPERS,
CORED, DESEEDED AND
CUT IN STRIPS

TOMATOES,
QUARTERED AND DESEEDED

For the dressing:

1 QUANTITY OF AÏOLI
(SEE PAGE 93)

Centre of Attraction

THE MAIN COURSE

Those with modest appetites may willingly

forego the third course. They may even

dispense with the first. But the main course

is always the star turn. The art of French

cookery is typified in the following recipes,

which make full use of wine, herbs

and garlic.

SERVES 4

25 G/1 OZ BUTTER

4 COD CUTLETS

1 ONION, CHOPPED

1 GARLIC CLOVE, CRUSHED

175 G/6 OZ MUSHROOMS,
SLICED

250 G/ 8 OZ TOMATOES,
SKINNED, DESEEDED AND DICED

5 TABLESPOONS DRY WHITE WINE

SALT AND FRESHLY GROUND
BLACK PEPPER

1 TABLESPOON CHOPPED FRESH
FLAT LEAF PARSLEY

CABILLAUD À LA MISTRAL

Cod is a favourite fish all over Europe.
In France, it is called 'cabillaud' when fresh, and
'morue' when salted.

Melt the butter in a frying pan, add the cod cutlets and cook gently for about 10 minutes, turning once. Transfer the fish to a serving dish and keep hot.

Add the onion and garlic to the pan and cook slowly until the onion has softened but not coloured. Add the mushrooms and tomatoes and cook for a further 3 minutes. Stir in the white wine, bring to the boil and simmer for about 5 minutes. Check the seasoning, pour the sauce over the cutlets, scatter with chopped fresh parsley, and serve.

VARIATIONS

Any meaty fish can be substituted in this dish. Salmon, for instance, suits tomato recipes perfectly. I would garnish it with chopped fresh basil, since basil also marries well with tomato. Other firm-fleshed fish, such as hake, halibut, haddock and monkfish, may also be used.

PREVIOUS PAGES *Poule au Pot made with Guinea Fowl, with its soup (recipe pages 54-55).*

Fresh Salmon with Prawns

Salmon makes an excellent dish for special occasions, served either hot or cold. This recipe serves six people, but is easily adapted for a larger party and larger fish.

Serves 6

1.25 kg/2½ lb tail piece of salmon

150 ml/¼ pint dry white wine

300 ml/½ pint water

1 bay leaf

2 sprigs parsley

6 peppercorns

To garnish

½ cucumber, thinly sliced

175 g/6 oz shelled prawns, sliced in half lengthways, if large

sprigs of fresh dill

Put the salmon in a large, buttered, ovenproof dish with the other ingredients. Cover the dish with a lid or foil, and cook in a preheated oven at 160°C (325°F) Gas Mark 3 for 30 minutes, basting frequently. Check that the centre is cooked – the flesh along the backbone should be opaque when tested with a fork. When cooked, remove the fish from the oven and leave to cool in the dish. Baste occasionally.

When cool, carefully slip off the skin. Divide the fish in half by sliding a sharp knife along both sides of the flat backbone. Discard the bones. Arrange on a large serving dish, putting a tail end at each end of the dish. Chill.

Arrange the cucumber slices, overlapping slightly, around the edge of the salmon. Place the prawns in a row down the middle, alternating with sprigs of dill. Serve with a dish of Mayonnaise (see page 93).

Variation

Poached Salmon with Hollandaise Sauce: follow the recipe above, but do not allow to cool. Carefully slip off the skin, and moisten the fish with a little of the basting liquid. Serve hot, with boiled new potatoes scattered with chopped fresh dill, and Hollandaise Sauce (see page 92).

1.1 KG/2¼ LB SEA BASS, GUTTED
AND WITH GILLS REMOVED

4 SPRIGS FRESH TARRAGON

1 LEMON, SLICED

2 TABLESPOONS DRY WHITE WINE

SALT AND FRESHLY GROUND
BLACK PEPPER

CHOPPED FRESH THYME LEAVES
OR FLAT LEAF PARSLEY,
TO GARNISH

For the lemon butter sauce

1 TABLESPOON PLAIN FLOUR

JUICE OF ½ LEMON

1 SMALL EGG YOLK

45 G/1½ OZ BUTTER, MELTED

150 ML/5 FL OZ SINGLE CREAM

SALT AND FRESHLY GROUND
BLACK PEPPER

2 TABLESPOONS CHOPPED FRESH
TARRAGON OR PARSLEY

BAKED SEA BASS

In France, whole fish are often cooked simply in this way. You can substitute any other good-quality fish – the only rule is that it should be the best, and very fresh.

Wash the sea bass thoroughly and pat dry with paper towels. Place a sheet of foil on a large baking tray and oil it lightly. Place the sea bass on the foil and tuck tarragon, slices of lemon and seasoning inside the belly of the fish. Season the outside.

Bring up the sides of the foil, then sprinkle over the wine and close the parcel. Bake the sea bass in a preheated oven at 200°C (400°F) Gas Mark 6 for 30 minutes, or until the flesh is opaque and flakes easily.

Carefully lift the fish on to a warmed serving plate, pour over the cooking juices, sprinkle with chopped fresh thyme or parsley and serve at once with the lemon butter sauce.

To make the lemon butter sauce

Whisk all the ingredients together, except the seasoning and tarragon or parsley. Transfer the mixture to a small saucepan and heat very gently, stirring constantly until the mixture thickens enough to coat the back of a spoon. Season to taste, stir in the herbs, and pour into a sauceboat to serve.

TROUT WITH ALMONDS

SERVES 4

50 G/2 OZ BUTTER

50 G/2 OZ BLANCHED ALMONDS,
SHREDDED

4 TROUT, CLEANED

SALT AND FRESHLY GROUND
BLACK PEPPER

To garnish

4 BLACK OLIVES, PITTED

A FEW SPRIGS OF
FLAT LEAF PARSLEY

'Truites aux Amandes' is a classic trout recipe – the crunchy almonds contrasting deliciously with the smooth creamy fish. Other traditional recipes include 'Truite à la Meunière' (the miller's wife!), in which the trout is dusted with flour and fried in butter, and 'Truite au Bleu', in which very fresh fish are poached in a court bouillon.

Melt the butter in a frying pan, add the almonds and fry them gently until golden brown. Remove the almonds from the pan.

Meanwhile wash and dry the trout, remove the fins, eyes and part of the tails but leave the heads on. Fry the trout in the butter remaining in the pan, allowing about 5 minutes for each side, according to size. Season to taste.

Arrange the trout on a hot serving dish with a black olive in the eye of each. Sprinkle with the almonds and pour over the butter from the pan. Garnish with the sprigs of parsley.

VARIATION

Truite à la Meunière: prepare the trout as in the recipe above, then dust it with 2 tablespoons seasoned flour and fry in about 50 g/2 oz butter with 1 tablespoon vegetable oil added. Allow 5 minutes for each side.

Melt about 50 g/2 oz butter, or more to taste, in a small saucepan. Serve the fish, with the melted butter poured over.

12 FILLETS OF LEMON SOLE

40 G/1½ OZ BUTTER

JUICE OF ½ LEMON

FRESHLY GROUND BLACK PEPPER

1 TEASPOON CHOPPED FRESH
DILL, TO GARNISH

For the sauce

½ CUCUMBER, PEELED AND
DESEEDED

150 ML/¼ PINT MAYONNAISE
(SEE PAGE 93)

150 ML/¼ PINT DOUBLE CREAM,
LIGHTLY WHIPPED

JUICE OF ½ LEMON

1 TEASPOON CHOPPED FRESH
DILL

SALT AND FRESHLY GROUND
BLACK PEPPER

SOLE WITH LEMON AND CUCUMBER SAUCE

One of the most prized of all sea fish, sole gets its name from the Romans, who also loved it. They called it 'Solea Jovi' – 'Jupiter's Sandal'. In this recipe, the fish is baked in the oven, but you could also fry it 'à la Meunière', as described in the previous recipe for trout.

Butter a 900 ml/1½ pint shallow ovenproof dish. Place the fish in the dish, dot with the butter and sprinkle over the lemon juice and pepper. Cover with foil and bake at 160°C (325°F) Gas Mark 3 for about 25 minutes, until the fish flakes easily.

Cut the cucumber in 5 mm/¼ inch dice, sprinkle thickly with salt and leave for 15 minutes. Rinse the cucumber in cold water, then pat dry with kitchen paper. Blend the mayonnaise, whipped cream, lemon juice and seasonings together, then add the cucumber and chopped dill.

Arrange the fish on a hot serving dish, sprinkle with more chopped dill, to garnish, and serve with the sauce.

COQ AU VIN

Coq au Vin is one of the great French classics, usually made with red wine. It is also excellent with white wine, which perhaps gives the dish a lighter, more 'summery' flavour. Use the liver in a different dish – perhaps sliced, fried with mushrooms in butter, and served on toast.

Melt 25 g/1 oz of the butter in a pan with the olive oil and fry the bacon cubes until golden brown. Remove the bacon from the pan and drain on kitchen paper. Fry the chicken in the same pan until brown, turning once.

Put the chicken joints into a 1.8 litre/3 pint flameproof casserole, then add the bacon. Fry the shallots and celery in the fat remaining in the pan until softened but not coloured, then add to the casserole. Melt the remaining butter in the pan, add the mushrooms, sauté for 2 minutes, then put to one side, on kitchen paper.

Blend the garlic and flour with the fat remaining in the pan. Cook gently until browned, stirring frequently. Add the wine, chicken stock, herbs and seasoning to taste. Simmer until the mixture has thickened. Pour over the chicken joints in the casserole and add the giblets. Bring to the boil, cover and cook in a preheated oven at 160°C (325°F) Gas Mark 3 for about 45 minutes until tender.

When almost tender remove the giblets and herbs from the casserole. Stir in the sautéed mushrooms and cook for a further 10 minutes. Skim off any excess fat with absorbent kitchen paper. Check the seasoning. Serve, garnished with fried bread triangles.

SERVES 6

40 G/1½ OZ BUTTER

1 TABLESPOON OLIVE OIL

125 G/4 OZ PIECE SMOKED STREAKY BACON, CUBED

1.5-2 KG/3-4 LB CHICKEN, JOINTED

12 SHALLOTS

2 CELERY STICKS, FINELY CHOPPED

175 G/6 OZ BUTTON MUSHROOMS

2 FAT GARLIC CLOVES, CRUSHED

2 TABLESPOONS PLAIN FLOUR

450 ML/¾ PINT RED BURGUNDY

150 ML/¼ PINT CHICKEN STOCK

2 SPRIGS FRESH THYME

2 BAY LEAVES

A FEW PARSLEY STALKS

SALT AND FRESHLY GROUND BLACK PEPPER

THE CHICKEN GIBLETS (EXCEPT THE LIVER), WASHED

SMALL TRIANGLES OF FRIED BREAD, TO GARNISH

1.5-2 KG/3½-4 LB CHICKEN

½ LEMON

3 CARROTS, QUARTERED

1 ONION, QUARTERED

1 BAY LEAF

2 SPRIGS OF FLAT LEAF PARSLEY

450 ML/¾ PINT CHICKEN STOCK

150 ML/¼ PINT WHITE WINE

SALT AND FRESHLY GROUND
BLACK PEPPER

For the sauce

25 G/1 OZ BUTTER

25 G/1 OZ PLAIN FLOUR

2 TABLESPOONS CHOPPED
FRESH TARRAGON

2 EGG YOLKS

75 ML/3 FL OZ SINGLE CREAM

SALT AND FRESHLY GROUND
BLACK PEPPER

TARRAGON CHICKEN

*Tarragon and chicken – like tomato and basil, and
asparagus and Hollandaise – is one of those 'marriages made
in heaven'. Tarragon is also good with French Roast Chicken (see
page 51) – before cooking, gently pull the skin away from the breast
and insert a little butter and chopped tarragon. Roast, with a bunch
of tarragon in the cavity of the chicken. Don't forget to make
gravy with this version – it is deliciously aromatic.*

Place the chicken into a flameproof casserole with the giblets (excluding the liver) and the first group of ingredients. Cover the casserole, and simmer for about 1¼ hours or until tender. Remove the bird from the casserole, skin and joint it and, if liked, remove the bones. Keep the chicken hot.

Strain the cooking liquid into a clean pan and then reduce it to 450 ml/¾ pint. Heat the butter in a pan, blend in the flour and cook for 1 minute. Add the chicken liquor and bring to the boil, stirring. Add the tarragon and simmer for 3 minutes.

Blend the egg yolks and cream together, then add about 4 tablespoons of the sauce to the egg mixture and return it to the pan. Return the chicken pieces to the pan and heat through, without simmering, for 5 minutes. Check seasoning and serve immediately.

CHICKEN WITH PRUNES

This dish is equally good made with rabbit in a traditional dish from the Périgord, 'Lapin aux Pruneaux'.

4 CHICKEN JOINTS

125 G/4 OZ PRUNES

1 ONION, SLICED

1 BAY LEAF

6 PEPPERCORNS

300 ML/½ PINT RED WINE

2 TABLESPOONS OLIVE OIL

25 G/1 OZ BUTTER

4 ONIONS, QUARTERED

2 TABLESPOONS PLAIN FLOUR

150 ML/¼ PINT CHICKEN STOCK

1 ROUNDED TABLESPOON
REDCURRANT JELLY

SALT AND FRESHLY GROUND
BLACK PEPPER

Place the chicken joints in a bowl with the prunes, sliced onion, bay leaf, peppercorns and wine, and marinate in the refrigerator overnight. Next day, strain the marinade, stone the prunes and reserve the liquid, the chicken and the prunes. Pat the chicken dry on kitchen paper.

Heat the oil in a large frying pan or heavy-based casserole. Add the butter, then the chicken joints and fry quickly until golden brown, turning once. Remove the chicken from the pan, add the quartered onions, fry until golden then add to the chicken.

Blend the flour with the fat remaining in the pan, stir in the liquid from the marinade, and bring to boiling point, stirring. Add the remaining ingredients to the pan, followed by the chicken, onions and prunes. Cover and simmer gently for about 30 minutes until the chicken is tender. Check the seasoning, and serve.

SERVES 4

2 TABLESPOONS OLIVE OIL

25 G/1 OZ BUTTER

4 CHICKEN JOINTS

25 G/1 OZ PLAIN FLOUR

300 ML/½ PINT DRY WHITE WINE

300 ML/½ PINT CHICKEN STOCK
OR WATER

425 G/14 OZ CANNED PLUM
TOMATOES

50 G/2 OZ BUTTON
MUSHROOMS, SLICED

3 FAT GARLIC CLOVES, CRUSHED

A BOUQUET GARNI
(SEE PAGE 122)

SALT AND FRESHLY GROUND
BLACK PEPPER

CHICKEN MARENGO

This famous dish has an interesting history. It was created for Napoleon by his chef Dunand after his victory over the Austrians at the Battle of Marengo in Italy, in 1800. It was reputedly served to him on the actual battlefield, and the original included chicken, tomato, garlic, brandy, crayfish and fried eggs!

Heat the oil in a large pan. Add the butter and, when melted, the chicken. Fry the chicken joints quickly until golden brown, turning once. Lift the chicken out on to a plate.

Add the flour to the fat in the pan and allow to brown slightly. Reduce the heat, add the wine and stock or water, and stir until thickened. Add the remaining ingredients and the chicken to the pan and stir well.

Simmer very slowly until the chicken is tender – about 30 minutes. Check the seasoning and remove the bouquet garni before serving.

CHICKEN OLIVES

Each boned piece of chicken is stuffed with seasoned butter, wrapped in ham and then baked in a cheese sauce. Use chicken breasts instead for a special occasion.

Blend together the butter, lemon rind and parsley, season to taste, and use to stuff the cavities of the chicken pieces. Wrap each piece in a slice of ham.

Place in a shallow ovenproof dish, close together, in order to prevent the ham from unrolling. Cover with the béchamel sauce, blended with two-thirds of the cheese. Sprinkle with the remaining cheese and cook in a preheated oven at 190°C (375°F) Gas Mark 5 for about 30 minutes.

VARIATIONS

Veal Olives, Turkey Olives, Pork Olives and **Beef Olives**: replace the chicken with a similar quantity of veal, turkey or pork escalopes or beef fillet. Place them between 2 sheets of clingfilm and flatten with a rolling pin. Place a spoonful of stuffing on one-half of each escalope or fillet, fold over, and wrap each one in a slice of ham. Proceed as in the main recipe.

SERVES 6

50 G/2 OZ BUTTER

RIND OF 1 LEMON

2 TABLESPOONS CHOPPED FRESH PARSLEY

12 SKINNED AND BONED CHICKEN THIGHS

12 SLICES THINLY CUT HAM

300 ML/½ PINT BÉCHAMEL SAUCE AT COATING CONSISTENCY (SEE PAGE 90)

75 G/3 OZ GRATED GRUYÈRE CHEESE

SALT AND FRESHLY GROUND BLACK PEPPER

FRENCH ROAST CHICKEN

The chicken is roasted with a little stock added to the roasting pan. This method keeps the bird moist, and makes the skin very crisp.

SERVES 4

3 SPRIGS OF FRESH THYME

125 G/4 OZ BUTTER, SOFTENED

1.6-1.8 KG/3½-4 LB OVEN-READY
FREE-RANGE CHICKEN,
WITH GIBLETS

300 ML/½ PINT CHICKEN STOCK,
MADE FROM THE GIBLETS

8 CHICKEN LIVERS

2 TEASPOONS PLAIN FLOUR

1 TEASPOON FRESH THYME
LEAVES, TO GARNISH

SALT AND FRESHLY GROUND
BLACK PEPPER

*Illustrated opposite,
together with Baked Garlic
(recipe page 89).*

Stuff the thyme and 30 g/1 oz of the butter into the chicken and season with black pepper. Tie the legs together to neaten the shape. Put aside 30 g/1 oz of the butter and spread the remaining butter over the breast of the bird.

Place the chicken, breast-side down, in a small roasting tin and pour over the stock. Cook in a preheated oven at 200°C (400°F) Gas Mark 6 for 20 minutes per pound, or 40 minutes per kilo, plus 20 minutes extra. During roasting, turn the chicken on to each of its sides, and finally on to its breast to brown all over. Baste occasionally. Should the bird brown too quickly, cover it loosely with foil.

Test the chicken towards the end of the cooking time by inserting a fine skewer into the thickest part of the thigh – the juices will run clear when the chicken is cooked.

Fry the chicken livers in the reserved 30 g/1 oz of butter for about 4 minutes, turning all the time.

Remove the chicken from the roasting tin, sprinkle with pepper and thyme leaves, and keep it warm on a serving plate. To make the gravy, pour the juices from the roasting tin into a jug and reserve, leaving about 1 tablespoon of fat in the tin. Stir the flour in to the fat, and cook until lightly browned. Add the reserved stock and bring to the boil, stirring. Check the seasoning, strain the gravy into a gravy boat and serve the livers with the chicken and the gravy.

Baked Garlic (page 89) and Lyonnaise Potatoes (page 84) would be suitable accompaniments.

SERVES 6

6 SKINNED AND BONED CHICKEN
BREASTS

2 TABLESPOONS SEASONED
PLAIN FLOUR

1 EGG, BEATEN

3 ROUNDED TABLESPOONS
BROWN BREADCRUMBS

OIL FOR DEEP FRYING

LEMON WEDGES, TO SERVE

For the herbed butter

75 G/3 OZ BUTTER, SOFTENED

2 TEASPOONS LEMON JUICE

2 TEASPOONS CHOPPED PARSLEY

1 TEASPOON CHOPPED FRESH
TARRAGON

CHICKEN ESCALOPES

To make the herbed butter

Blend all the ingredients together. Place on a piece of foil, form into a sausage shape, roll up in the foil, and chill.

To make the escalopes

Place the chicken breasts between 2 sheets of clingfilm, and flatten gently with a rolling pin.

Coat the breasts in flour, then with egg and breadcrumbs. Heat the oil in a large deep pan. Add the breasts and fry for about 5 minutes. Drain on kitchen paper and served with slices of herbed butter, wedges of lemon and a green salad.

VARIATIONS

This recipe is equally delicious made with other meats.

Veal Escalopes: substitute 6 veal escalopes for the chicken breasts, and use finely chopped marjoram instead of tarragon in the herbed butter.

Pork Escalopes: substitute 6 pork escalopes for the chicken breasts, and 1 teaspoon chopped fresh sage or basil instead of the chopped tarragon in the herbed butter.

Turkey Escalopes: special cuts of turkey are now becoming widely available, and would be delicious in this recipe. Substitute 6 turkey escalopes for the chicken breasts, and about 1 teaspoon of chopped fresh rosemary leaves or thyme leaves, instead of the chopped tarragon in the herbed butter.

DUCK À L'ORANGE

Watercress and an orange salad – sliced oranges in a dressing made from orange juice, wine vinegar and oil – are the classic accompaniments for this dish.

Sprinkle the duck inside and out with salt and pepper. Place on a rack or trivet in a meat tin, and prick the body all over with a fork. Cook in a preheated oven at 180°C (350°F) Gas Mark 4 for 1½ hours, or until done. Start with the breast-side down, until browned, and then turn the bird on its back.

To make the stock, cover the duck neck and giblets (except the liver) with water and cook until tender. Strain and reserve 300 ml/½ pint stock.

Pour off the duck fat from the roasting tin and reserve for future use. Brush the duck with the honey, and roast for a further 30 minutes.

Put 4 tablespoons duck fat in a pan, then blend in the flour. Stir in the reserved stock, orange juice and wine. Simmer until the sauce has been reduced by one-third. Add the redcurrant jelly and stir until dissolved. Check seasoning.

Put the duck on a hot serving dish. Spoon over a little of the sauce and serve the rest separately. Garnish with orange slices and sprigs of watercress.

The reserved duck fat can be used to fry other dishes, such as the Garlic Fried Potatoes on page 84.

SERVES 4

1 DUCK, ABOUT 2.25-2.5 KG/4½-5 LB, WITH GIBLETS

2 TABLESPOONS CLEAR HONEY

25 G/1 OZ PLAIN FLOUR

150 ML/¼ PINT FRESH ORANGE JUICE

150 ML/¼ PINT RED WINE

1 TABLESPOON REDCURRANT JELLY

SALT AND FRESHLY GROUND BLACK PEPPER

To garnish

1 ORANGE, THINLY SLICED

A BUNCH OF WATERCRESS

1 GOOD-SIZED GUINEA FOWL,
OR A 1.5 KG/3 LB CHICKEN

½ CABBAGE

2 LEEKS, TRIMMED, SPLIT
AND WASHED THOROUGHLY

1 STICK CELERY

3 TABLESPOONS OLIVE OIL

4 ONIONS, STUCK WITH CLOVES

4 CARROTS

4 PARSNIPS OR TURNIPS

A BOUQUET GARNI

RIND AND JUICE OF ½ ORANGE
(OPTIONAL)

1 LARGE SKINNED TOMATO
(OPTIONAL)

600 ML/1 PINT WHITE WINE

600 ML/1 PINT CHICKEN STOCK
OR 300 ML/½ PINT
CHICKEN STOCK AND
300 ML/½ PINT VEAL STOCK

2 TABLESPOONS CHOPPED
FRESH, FLAT LEAF PARSLEY,
TO GARNISH

For the stuffing

1 ONION, CHOPPED

1 GARLIC CLOVE, CRUSHED

1 TABLESPOON OLIVE OIL
OR 30 G/1 OZ BUTTER

2 RASHERS BACON, CHOPPED

4 SLICES STALE BREAD, CRUSTS
REMOVED, TORN INTO LARGE
PIECES, SPRINKLED WITH MILK,
AND SQUEEZED DRY

2 TABLESPOONS CHOPPED FRESH
HERBS, SUCH AS FLAT LEAF
PARSLEY, AND TARRAGON,
ROSEMARY OR THYME

1 EGG, BEATEN

POULE AU POT MADE WITH GUINEA FOWL

'Poule au Pot', or 'Chicken in the Pot' is the famous French dish that King Henri IV hoped all his subjects could have every Sunday. It was traditionally made with a boiling chicken – a rare bird these days. Boiling chickens would be cooked for 3 hours or more – but a young, oven-ready bird will only take about 1½ hours. 'Poule au Pot' is a little more 'gamey' made with guinea fowl ('pintade' in French). Traditionally, the vegetables are cooked in the pot with the chicken, but if preferred, add them for the last 30 minutes only.

To make the stuffing

Fry the onion and garlic in the oil or butter until golden. Grill or fry the bacon until crispy. Mix them all together with the other the stuffing ingredients.

To prepare the guinea fowl

Loosen the skin of the bird around the neck end, and pack the stuffing loosely into the neck. Secure the neck with skewers, and truss the bird with string. If any stuffing remains, tie it up in muslin, and poach it with the bird.

To cook

Tie up the cabbage with trussing string – if your casserole is small, cut it into two quarters so it fits into the pot better. Tie the leeks and celery together.

Heat the oil in a large flameproof casserole, and brown the guinea fowl on all sides. Remove and set aside. Add the onions, carrots, parsnips or turnips, and brown gently in the oil. Return the guinea fowl to the casserole and pack all the browned vegetables tightly around it. Tuck in the bouquet garni, the 'trussed' cabbage, leeks and celery. Add the tomato and the rind and juice of the orange, if using. Include the extra stuffing tied up in muslin.

Pour over the wine, and enough chicken stock to cover all the ingredients. Bring to the boil, reduce the heat and simmer on top of the stove, or in the oven at 160°C, 325°F, Gas Mark 3, for about 2 hours, or until the guinea fowl is cooked and the vegetables tender. Add more stock or water as necessary to keep the bird covered.

Illustrated on pages 38-39

To serve

Remove the bouquet garni and orange rind (if using). Remove the guinea fowl from the pot, remove and discard trussing strings, carve into joints and slice the stuffing.

Place on a serving plate and surround with the poached vegetables. Spoon over a little of the cooking liquid to keep the dish moist. Sprinkle with chopped parsley and serve, accompanied by boiled new potatoes, a little extra stock in a sauceboat, and a bowl of Mayonnaise or Aïoli (see page 93).

Traditionally, the strained stock was served first as a soup, often enriched with rice or pasta, or simply sprinkled over with chopped fresh parsley or chives, and accompanied by good crusty bread. This is delicious – but only if your guests have very large appetites!

SERVES 6

250 G/8 OZ DRIED OR FROZEN
CHESTNUTS

3 TABLESPOONS OLIVE OIL

25 G/1 OZ BUTTER

3 PLUMP PIGEONS, EACH SPLIT
IN HALF

2 TABLESPOONS PLAIN FLOUR

300 ML/½ PINT BEAUJOLAIS OR
OTHER LIGHT RED WINE

300 ML/½ PINT CHICKEN STOCK

250 G/8 OZ ONIONS,
QUARTERED

THE RIND AND JUICE OF
1 ORANGE

1 TEASPOON REDCURRANT JELLY

A BOUQUET GARNI

SALT AND FRESHLY GROUND
BLACK PEPPER

SPRIGS OF FLAT LEAF PARSLEY,
TO GARNISH

PIGEON CASSEROLE WITH CHESTNUTS

If using dried chestnuts, soak them overnight, then drain and pat dry with kitchen towels.

Heat 2 tablespoons of the olive oil in a pan, add the butter then the pigeons and fry until browned, turning once. Transfer the birds to a 2.4 litre/4 pint casserole. Add the remaining oil to the pan and add the chestnuts. Fry until evenly browned, then drain on kitchen paper.

Add the flour to the pan, stir, and cook gently until brown. Stir in the wine and stock. Bring to the boil, then pour the sauce into the casserole. Add all the other ingredients except the chestnuts and the sprigs of parsley.

Cover and cook in a preheated oven at 160°C (325°F) Gas Mark 3 for about 1½-2 hours or until tender. Add the chestnuts about 45 minutes before the end of the cooking time. Remove the bouquet garni and orange rind. Check the seasoning and garnish with sprigs of parsley before serving.

NORMANDY PHEASANT

A favourite recipe which can be prepared ahead and reheated. Apples, Calvados, butter and cream are ingredients typical of Normandy. This recipe doesn't include the cream, so you could serve the pheasant with the Potatoes Dauphinois recipe which appears on page 85.

Measure the oil and butter into a large frying pan. Fry the pheasants on all sides until brown, then lift out into a deep casserole just large enough to take them.

In the fat left in the pan, fry the onion until golden. Add the flour, mix well and gradually blend in the wine and stock, stirring until thickened. Add the redcurrant jelly, chopped apple and seasoning.

Pour the sauce over the pheasants, cover and cook in a preheated oven at 160°C (325°F) Gas Mark 3 for about 1 hour. Younger birds will be tender in this time. For older birds, lift them out of the sauce, and, if the breast is done, carve off the legs and return them to cook for a little longer in the sauce. Wrap the carcass and breast in foil to keep them moist, and keep warm. Before serving, cut the birds into serving pieces, and return to the sauce to reheat.

Warm the Calvados or brandy in a small saucepan or ladle, pour over the pheasants and light with a match. Shake the pan gently until the flames subside.

Serve, garnished with slices of fried apple and sprigs of flat leaf parsley.

SERVES 4

1 TABLESPOON SUNFLOWER OIL

25 G/1 OZ BUTTER

BRACE OF YOUNG, OVEN-READY PHEASANTS

1 LARGE ONION, CHOPPED

A GENEROUS 25 G/1 OZ PLAIN FLOUR

150 ML/¼ PINT WHITE WINE

300 ML/½ PINT GAME OR CHICKEN STOCK

2 TABLESPOONS REDCURRANT JELLY

1 LARGE BRAMLEY COOKING APPLE, PEELED, CORED AND CHOPPED

2 TABLESPOONS CALVADOS OR BRANDY

SALT AND FRESHLY GROUND BLACK PEPPER

To garnish

2 COX'S OR OTHER DESSERT APPLES, CORED, SLICED AND FRIED IN BUTTER

SPRIGS OF FLAT LEAF PARSLEY

For the marinade

300 ML / ½ PINT RED WINE

4 TABLESPOONS OLIVE OIL

4 SPRIGS OF FLAT LEAF PARSLEY

1 SPRIG FRESH THYME

3 FAT GARLIC CLOVES, CRUSHED

1 ONION, CHOPPED

For the filling

750 G / 1½ LB BONED RABBIT
PIECES

2 TABLESPOONS PLAIN FLOUR

SALT AND FRESHLY GROUND
BLACK PEPPER

4 TABLESPOONS OLIVE OIL

125 G / 4 OZ BACON, DICED

300 ML / ½ PINT CHICKEN STOCK

250 G / 8 OZ BABY ONIONS

SHORTCRUST PASTRY MADE WITH
175 G / 6 OZ PLAIN FLOUR
(SEE PAGE 26)

Illustrated opposite

RABBIT PIE

Mix the ingredients for the marinade in a bowl. Add the pieces of boned rabbit, cover and leave in the refrigerator for about 12 hours, turning occasionally. Drain the rabbit, reserving the marinade, and dry on kitchen paper.

Mix together the flour, salt and pepper and use to coat the rabbit pieces. Heat the oil in a pan, and fry the diced bacon until brown. Remove and reserve. Add the rabbit to the pan and fry until golden brown. Add the marinade and stock, bring to the boil, cover and simmer for about 1½ hours or until tender. Add the onions after 1 hour. Put the meat and cooking liquid in a 1.2 litre/2 pint ovenproof dish with the bacon. Leave until cold.

Make Shortcrust Pastry (see page 26), and use to cover the pie dish. Chill for about 15 minutes, and cook in a preheated oven at 200°C (400°F) Gas Mark 6 for 30 minutes or until the top is golden brown.

VARIATION

Chicken Pie or **Game Pie**: this recipe is also good made with chicken or other game, such as pheasant. Replace the rabbit with 750 g/1½ lb of boned chicken thighs or pheasant. Marinate the chicken with tarragon, rather than thyme.

125 G/4 OZ ROQUEFORT
CHEESE, CRUMBLED

30 G/1 OZ BUTTER, SOFTENED

60 G/2 OZ WALNUT PIECES,
ROUGHLY CHOPPED

4 BEEF TOURNEDOS,
ABOUT 125 G/4 OZ EACH

FRESHLY GROUND BLACK PEPPER

BEEF TOURNEDOS

Cut from the eye of the fillet, tournedos are extravagant, but there is no waste. They should be 2.5-4 cm/1-1½ inches thick, and weigh about 125 g/4 oz each.

Mix the cheese, butter and walnuts in a small bowl and season with freshly ground black pepper. Preheat the grill to hot.

Place the tournedos on to a grill rack and season. Grill for about 6-7 minutes for rare steak, 10 minutes for medium and 15 minutes for well done, turning once.

Two minutes before they are ready, spead the cheese and nut mixture on to the tournedos and flash back under the grill until the cheese has melted.

Serve at once with new potatoes and a crisp green salad.

VARIATIONS

Tournedos with Mushrooms: omit the cheese, butter and walnuts. Grill the tournedos as in the main recipe.

Melt 25 g/1 oz butter in a small pan. Sauté 1 finely chopped onion until softened but not coloured. Add about 500 g/1 lb sliced chestnut mushrooms, and sauté until done. Add a little more butter if required. Swirl in 2-3 tablespoons crème fraîche, and serve, sprinkled with chopped fresh parsley, and accompanied by creamy mashed potatoes.

Tournedos with Butter Sauce: grill the tournedos on a sheet of kitchen foil. Melt 50 g/2 oz butter in a small pan, add the juice of ½ lemon, the juices from the foil, and 1 tablespoon finely chopped fresh parsley. Serve, accompanied by creamy mashed potatoes, to soak up the buttery juices.

BOEUF EN CROÛTE

Cook the beef fillet first, then chill, wrap in pastry, glaze and bake until golden. This is an excellent dish to choose for a dinner party, because you can prepare it and leave it in the refrigerator for up to 24 hours before final cooking.

SERVES 4-6

50 G/2 OZ BUTTER

900 G/2 LB BEEF FILLET, CUT FROM THE CENTRE OF THE FILLET

2 LARGE ONIONS, SLICED

100G/4 OZ MUSHROOMS, SLICED

425 G/14 OZ FROZEN PUFF PASTRY, THAWED

BEATEN EGG, TO GLAZE

SALT AND FRESHLY GROUND BLACK PEPPER

Melt the butter in a roasting tin. Trim any fat off the fillet, and roll the meat in the melted butter. Roast in a preheated oven at 220°C (425°F) Gas Mark 7 for about 20 minutes, turning the meat over once so that it browns on both sides. Remove to a plate and cool completely.

Add the onion to the juices in the tin, and cook, stirring, until golden. Add the mushrooms and cook for 2 minutes more. Remove from the heat, season and set aside to cool.

Roll out the pastry to a rectangle 35 x 40 cm/14 x 16 inches depending on the size of the meat. Place half the mushroom mixture down the centre of the pastry then place the meat on top, flat side uppermost. Season well. Cut a 3.5 cm/1½ inch square from each corner of the pastry for decoration and keep on one side. Fold the pastry around the meat, so that it is completely sealed inside. Turn over and stand on a baking sheet. Brush liberally with beaten egg. Use the leftover pastry to decorate the top with leaves or lattice. You can chill it for up to 24 hours in the refrigerator before final cooking.

Preheat the oven to 220°C (425°F) Gas Mark 7 for about 25-30 minutes until pale golden brown. Make a gravy from the reserved onions and mushrooms to serve with the beef.

SERVES 4-6

750 G/1½ LB CHUCK STEAK

25 G/1 OZ BACON FAT
OR OLIVE OIL

1765 G/6 OZ UNSMOKED
RINDLESS STREAKY BACON, CUT
IN STRIPS 1 CM/½ INCH WIDE

25 G/1 OZ PLAIN FLOUR

300 ML/½ PINT BEEF STOCK

150 ML/¼ PINT RED WINE

A BOUQUET GARNI
(SEE PAGE 122)

250 G/8 OZ SMALL, EVENLY
SIZED ONIONS, PEELED

50 G/2 OZ BUTTON MUSHROOMS

SALT AND FRESHLY GROUND
BLACK PEPPER

Illustrated opposite

BOEUF BOURGUIGNON

Cut the steak into 3.5 cm/1½ inch squares. Melt the bacon fat or olive oil in a fairly large pan and fry the bacon for a couple of minutes until it begins to brown. Lift the bacon out of the pan and into a 1.8 litre/3 pint casserole. Fry the steak in the fat remaining in the pan until it is brown all over.

Add the steak to the bacon in the casserole and pour off all but 2 tablespoons of the fat. Blend the flour with the fat and continue to cook until it has browned. Remove the pan from the heat and stir in stock and wine. Return the pan to the heat, bring the liquid to boiling point, and simmer until thickened.

Add the bouquet garni and seasoning, adding only a little of the salt, as the bacon may be salty. Pour the liquid over the meat, cover the casserole, bring to the boil and simmer gently in a preheated oven at 160°C (325°F) Gas Mark 3 for 1½ hours.

Add the onions and mushrooms to the casserole and cook it for a further hour until the meat is really tender. Check the seasoning and add more salt and pepper if necessary. Skim any fat off the surface and discard.

Like many slow-cooked meat dishes, Boeuf Bourguignon tastes even better the day after it is made. Place in the oven, preheated to 180°C (350°F) Gas Mark 4 for about 45 minutes, or until heated through. Serve with creamy mashed potatoes.

SERVES 6

25 G/1 OZ PLAIN FLOUR

2 TEASPOONS GROUND GINGER

1 KG/2 LB BRAISING BEEF IN
2.5 CM/1 INCH CUBES

3 TABLESPOONS OLIVE OIL

1 RED PEPPER, SLICED

500 G/16 OZ CANNED
FLAGEOLET BEANS

SALT AND FRESHLY GROUND
BLACK PEPPER

For the sauce

1 TEASPOON CHILLI SAUCE

250 G/8 OZ CANNED PLUM
TOMATOES

250 G/8 OZ CHESTNUT
MUSHROOMS, SLICED

1 TABLESPOON WORCESTERSHIRE
SAUCE

2 TABLESPOONS SOFT BROWN
SUGAR

2 TABLESPOONS WINE VINEGAR

2 GARLIC CLOVES, CRUSHED

1 BAY LEAF

POT AU FEU WITH BEEF
AND FLAGEOLET BEANS

The traditional Pot au Feu contains a number of different meats, and can include a whole chicken, shin of beef or veal, and large, thick cuts of meat, together with vegetables, herbs and flavourings. The soup is served first, followed by the sliced meats and vegetables, and accompanied by mustard, pickles, cornichons and redcurrant jelly. Understandably, it is always cooked for a very large number of people. This recipe is much more manageable, and serves 6.

Mix the flour, ginger and seasonings and use to coat the beef. Heat the olive oil in a large pan, add the beef and fry quickly until browned, turning once. Drain on kitchen paper then transfer to a 1.8 litre/3 pint ovenproof dish.

Combine all the ingredients for the sauce and pour over the meat. Cover the dish, and cook in a preheated oven at 160°C (325°F) Gas Mark 3 for about 2 hours or until the meat is tender. Add the red pepper and flageolet beans 30 minutes before the end of the cooking time.

FILET DE PORC CHASSEUR

SERVES 6

1 KG/2 LB PORK FILLET

2 TABLESPOONS OLIVE OIL

50 G/2 OZ BUTTER

250 G/8 OZ ONIONS, CHOPPED

250 G/8 OZ CHESTNUT
MUSHROOM, SLICED

50 G/2 OZ PLAIN FLOUR

300 ML/½ PINT BEEF STOCK

150 ML/¼ PINT WHITE WINE

SALT AND FRESHLY GROUND
BLACK PEPPER

'Chasseur' (or hunters') dishes consist of meat sautéed with mushrooms and onions, and sometimes shallots and tomatoes. This is one of the easiest and most delicious ways to cook pork, and uses beautiful chestnut mushrooms, which I think keep their shape well in cooking.

Cut the pork in 3.5 cm/1½ inch pieces. Heat the oil in a pan, brown the pork quickly in the oil then remove from the pan. Heat the butter in the pan, add the onions and cook slowly until soft. Add the mushrooms.

Sprinkle in the flour, add stock and wine. Bring to the boil then simmer for 2-3 minutes. Replace the pork in the pan and season with salt and pepper. Cover and simmer for 20 minutes until the pork is tender. Serve with puréed potatoes and a bright green vegetable.

VARIATIONS

Chicken Chasseur: substitute chicken breasts, chicken stock and button mushrooms. Add 1 tablespoon of tomato purée and 1 tablespoon of chopped tarragon.

Lamb Chasseur: substitute lamb loin chops and chicken or beef stock. Add 1 tablespoon tomato purée, 2 crushed garlic cloves and 1 tablespoon chopped rosemary.

75 G/3 OZ DRIED HARICOT
BEANS

75 G/3 OZ DRIED CHICKPEAS

4 PORK CHOPS, ABOUT
250 G/8 OZ EACH

30 ML/2 TABLESPOONS
OLIVE OIL

250 G/8 OZ SMOKED BACON IN
ONE PIECE, CUT INTO STRIPS

500 G/1 LB COARSE PORK
SAUSAGES

2 LARGE ONIONS, SLICED

2 CLOVES GARLIC, CRUSHED

300 ML/10 FL OZ CHICKEN
STOCK

1 TABLESPOON TOMATO PURÉE

30 ML/2 TABLESPOONS DRY
WHITE WINE

2 X 400 G/14 OZ CANS CHOPPED
TOMATOES

2 SPRIGS FRESH THYME

2 SPRIGS FRESH MARJORAM

A FEW PARSLEY STALKS

SALT AND FRESHLY GROUND
BLACK PEPPER

Illustrated opposite

PORK CASSOULET

*The word 'cassoulet' comes from 'casserole', the
earthenware pot in which Cassoulet is baked. This dish is best
made a day ahead, and then reheated.*

Soak the haricot beans and chickpeas overnight in plenty of
cold water. The next day, drain and discard the soaking water,
cover the beans and chickpeas with fresh cold water and bring
to the boil. Boil rapidly for the first 10 minutes, then simmer
for about 50 minutes or until the beans are tender. Drain.

Trim the pork chops of excess fat and skin. Heat the oil in
a large flameproof casserole and brown the pork on both
sides. Lift out and drain on kitchen towels. Add the bacon and
sausages to the casserole and fry until nicely brown all over.
Lift out, drain them on kitchen towels and cut the sausages
diagonally into thick slices. Pour off most of the fat from the
casserole, leaving about 15 ml/1 tablespoon.

Lower the heat and add the onions to the casserole. Cook
until they begin to soften and turn golden. Add the garlic,
stock, tomatoes, tomato purée, wine, beans and fresh herbs.
Bring to the boil and return the pork chops, bacon and sliced
sausages to the casserole. Season well, then bring back to the
boil and cook in the oven, preheated to 170°C (325°F) Gas
Mark 3 for about 1 hour until the pork is tender.

Taste and adjust the seasoning and serve with crusty bread
and a crisp green salad.

4 LEAN PORK CHOPS,
WITHOUT SKIN

40 G/1½ OZ BUTTER

250 G/8 OZ OYSTER
MUSHROOMS, SLICED

25 G/1 OZ PLAIN FLOUR

300 ML/½ PINT DRY WHITE WINE

1 TABLESPOON CHOPPED FRESH
CHIVES

150 ML/¼ PINT CRÈME FRAÎCHE

SALT AND FRESHLY GROUND
BLACK PEPPER

PORC À LA CRÈME

One of my favourite ways with pork – quick and easy and absolutely delicious. Oyster mushrooms give out quite a bit of juice and so are excellent for sauce-making. Crème fraîche, with its slightly lemony flavour, finishes the sauce beautifully.

Season the chops with salt and pepper. Cook under a medium grill for 10 minutes on a piece of foil, turning once, until crisp and brown. Save the juices on the foil. Place the chops on a serving dish and keep hot.

Melt the butter in a pan, add the mushrooms and fry them gently for about 3 minutes until soft. Remove the mushrooms and reserve. Sprinkle the flour into the juices, stir well and cook for about 1 minute. Blend in the juices from the foil, the wine and herbs. Simmer for another 2 minutes, stirring all the time. Add the crème fraîche and the reserved mushrooms, and check the seasoning. Reheat almost to boiling point.

Pour the sauce over the pork chops. Serve with buttered noodles and grilled tomatoes.

VARIATIONS

This recipe is equally good made with other meats. Try **Chicken à la Crème** using boned breasts of chicken, and **Veal à la Crème** using escalopes of veal. Substitute herbs such as tarragon or marjoram instead of the chives.

BAYONNE LAMB

A typical French country stew.

SERVES 4

1 KG/2 LB MIDDLE NECK OF
LAMB, CHOPPED

2 ONIONS, CUT IN WEDGES

2 LARGE CARROTS, SLICED

4 BABY TURNIPS, PEELED AND
KEPT WHOLE

1 BAY LEAF

1 TABLESPOON LEMON JUICE

1.2 LITRES/2 PINTS WATER

125 G/4 OZ SMALL MUSHROOMS,
SLICED

45 G/1½ OZ BUTTER

45 G/1½ OZ PLAIN FLOUR

1 EGG YOLK

150 G/5 OZ CRÈME FRAÎCHE

SALT AND FRESHLY GROUND
BLACK PEPPER

2 TABLESPOONS CHOPPED
PARSLEY, TO GARNISH

Put the lamb in a flameproof casserole with the onions, carrots, turnips, bay leaf, lemon juice, seasoning and water. Bring to boiling point, cover and simmer on top of the cooker, or in a preheated oven at 160°C (325°F) Gas Mark 3 for about 1½ hours or until tender. Twenty minutes before the end of the cooking time, add the mushrooms. Place the lamb and the vegetables in a serving dish and keep hot.

Reduce the cooking liquid to 600 ml/1 pint by boiling rapidly. Make a roux with the butter and flour, then add the cooking liquid and simmer for 5 minutes longer. Add more seasoning if necessary. Blend together the egg yolk and crème fraîche and add a little to the sauce. Return this mixture to the pan and re-heat. Pour the sauce over the meat and scatter with chopped parsley.

VARIATION

A famous version of this dish is **Navarin of Lamb**, which uses very small young vegetables. As well as those listed above, include 500 g/1 lb fresh peas or mangetout, 12 spring onions, and 250 g/8 oz small French beans. The lamb should be browned in a little butter, then simmered in chicken stock, rather than water, for 1½ hours. Blanch the vegetables for 5 minutes in boiling water before browning in butter, then simmering in stock for about 15 minutes. Put vegetables and meat together, and heat through. Remove to a serving platter and keep warm. Boil the stock until reduced and thickened, strain, pour over the meat and vegetables, and serve.

SERVES 8

2 KG/4 LB LEG OF LAMB,
TUNNEL BONED BUT NOT
OPENED OUT

25 G/1 OZ BUTTER

3-4 CLOVES GARLIC, CRUSHED

225 G/½ LB SPINACH AND A FEW
SORREL LEAVES (IF AVAILABLE),
COARSELY SHREDDED

50 G/2 OZ BREADCRUMBS

1 EGG

425 G/14 OZ PACKET OF
FROZEN SHORTCRUST PASTRY
OR FRESH PASTRY, MADE
ACCORDING TO THE RECIPE ON
PAGE 27

1 EGG, BEATEN WITH
1 TEASPOON WATER

SALT AND FRESHLY GROUND
BLACK PEPPER

Illustrated opposite

GIGOT D'AGNEAU EN CROÛTE

This is a delicious way of cooking lamb – splendid for a dinner party and perfect for Sunday lunch, with its bright green centre stuffed with spinach and sorrel. Ask the butcher to tunnel bone the leg, but not to open it out; there must be a cavity to receive the stuffing.

Trim the meat and discard any excess fat. Melt the butter, add the garlic and cook gently for 2-3 minutes. Do not allow to brown. Add the spinach, sorrel (if using), salt and pepper and stir well for about 1 minute. Turn out into a bowl and add the breadcrumbs. Allow to cool and add the egg. Mix well. If time permits, set it aside to become completely cold. Season the cavity in the joint with salt and pepper and fill with the spinach mixture. Secure with skewers as tightly as possible.

Weigh the joint and roast for 25 minutes per 500 g/1 lb plus an extra 25 minutes in a preheated oven at 200°C (400°F) Gas Mark 6. Remove it from the oven and allow to cool.

Roll out the pastry to form a rectangle large enough to cover the lamb. Wrap the meat in the pastry with the join underneath. Return the parcel to the meat tin and decorate with small leaves made from the pastry trimmings. Prick the pastry all over with a knife, and brush it with beaten egg. Bake at 190°C (375°F) Gas Mark 5 for about 45 minutes until the pastry is a rich golden colour and the meat is heated through.

To serve the lamb, cut and lift off the pastry in portions, then carve the meat in the usual way. Serve with a rich gravy, to which 200 ml/7 fl oz crème fraîche may also be added to increase the quantity.

750G/1½ LB BONED SHOULDER
VEAL IN 3.5 CM/1½ INCH PIECES

2 ONIONS, QUARTERED

2 LARGE CARROTS, QUARTERED

3 BAY LEAVES

A SPRIG OF PARSLEY

JUICE OF ½ LEMON

900 ML/1½ PINTS VEAL OR
LIGHT STOCK

175 G/6 OZ BUTTON
MUSHROOMS

40 G/1½ OZ BUTTER

40 G/1½ OZ PLAIN FLOUR

1 EGG YOLK

50 ML/¼ PINT SINGLE CREAM

SALT AND FRESHLY GROUND
BLACK PEPPER

1 TABLESPOON CHOPPED FRESH
FLAT LEAF PARSLEY, TO GARNISH

SERVES 4

75 G/3 OZ BUTTER

250 G/8 OZ FLAT, OPEN
MUSHROOMS, STALKS INTACT

8 LAMBS' KIDNEYS, SKINNED,
HALVED AND CORES REMOVED

1 LARGE ONION, SLICED

1 TABLESPOON PLAIN FLOUR

1 TEASPOON TOMATO PURÉE

150 ML/¼ PINT BORDEAUX OR
OTHER RED WINE

150 ML/¼ PINT BEEF STOCK

1 SPRIG OF PARSLEY

1 SPRIG OF THYME

1 BAY LEAF

1 TABLESPOON CHOPPED FRESH
PARSLEY, TO GARNISH

BLANQUETTE DE VEAU

Put the veal pieces in a pan with the onions, carrots, bay leaves, parsley, lemon juice, seasoning and stock. Bring to boiling point, cover and simmer for about 1½ hours or until the veal is tender. Thirty minutes before the end of the cooking time add the mushrooms. Arrange the veal and vegetables in a serving dish and keep hot.

Make a roux with the butter and flour. Reduce the cooking liquid to 600 ml/1 pint by boiling rapidly, then blend with the roux and simmer, stirring, for 5 minutes. Check the seasoning. Blend together the egg yolk and cream. Add a little of the sauce. Return the egg mixture to the pan and reheat but do not boil. Check seasoning, then pour the sauce over the meat and vegetables. Serve, sprinkled with parsley.

KIDNEYS IN RED WINE

Melt 25 g/1 oz butter in a pan and sauté the mushrooms on both sides until cooked. Remove with a slotted spoon and keep warm. Add the remaining butter, and brown the kidneys quickly. Remove from the pan and set aside.

Add the onion to the pan and fry until golden. Blend in the flour, cook for 1 minute, then add the tomato purée, wine and stock. Bring to the boil, stirring. Replace the kidneys in the pan with the herbs, cover and simmer for 5 minutes.

Check seasoning, discard the herbs and turn the kidney mixture out on to a serving dish. Arrange the mushrooms on top, with stalks uppermost. Sprinkle with parsley, and serve.

OXTAIL

*This dish is very much improved if allowed to cool,
then refrigerated overnight. Carefully lift off the layer of fat
and discard. Place turned vegetables about 3.5 cm/1½ inches long
on top of the meat and stock and reheat thoroughly in the oven until
the oxtail is hot, and the vegetables are tender. Suitable vegetables
include carrots, swedes, turnips, parsnips and
shallots or baby onions.*

SERVES 6

1.5 KG/3 LB OXTAIL, CUT INTO
SEGMENTS

2 TABLESPOONS OLIVE OIL

2 ONIONS, CHOPPED

2 LARGE CARROTS, CHOPPED

½ HEAD OF CELERY, CHOPPED

2 RASHERS STREAKY BACON,
CHOPPED

2 TABLESPOONS PLAIN FLOUR

2 BAY LEAVES

3 SPRIGS PARSLEY

6 PEPPERCORNS

1.2 LITRES/2 PINTS BEEF STOCK

SALT AND FRESHLY GROUND
BLACK PEPPER

Trim any excess fat from the pieces of oxtail. Heat the oil in an ovenproof casserole, add the oxtail and brown quickly on all sides, then remove with a slotted spoon and set aside. Add the vegetables and bacon to the oil and cook gently for 5 minutes. Blend in the flour, cook for 1 minute, then return the oxtail to the casserole with the remaining ingredients. Bring to the boil, cover and simmer for about 4 hours on top of the stove or in the oven, until the meat can be easily removed from the bones. Arrange on a serving dish and keep hot.

Strain the stock and discard the vegetables and herbs. Reduce the stock to about 450 ml/¾ pint, check the seasoning and pour over the oxtail. Serve with creamy mashed potatoes.

VARIATION

Another delicious alternative is to steep about 25 g/1 oz of dried mushrooms – such as cèpes or porcini – in boiling water for about 30 minutes, then add mushrooms and the strained steeping liquid to the casserole before reheating.

Vegetables and Salads

AND SAUCES AND DRESSINGS

In family meals in France and in restaurants which cater mainly for French customers, rather than visiting tourists, vegetables or salads are served as a separate course. Thus the full flavour of the dish can be savoured in isolation – a point worth remembering if the main course itself is highly flavoured. Among the recipes given here are several which could be served as a first course.

POTATO AND CELERY SALAD

SERVES 4-6

500 G/1 LB WAXY POTATOES

6 TABLESPOONS FRENCH
DRESSING (SEE PAGE 91)

1 SMALL HEAD OF CELERY,
CHOPPED

150 ML/¼ PINT MAYONNAISE
(SEE PAGE 93)

3 TABLESPOONS CHOPPED CHIVES

SALT AND FRESHLY GROUND
BLACK PEPPER

Boil the potatoes in salted water in the usual way, drain and peel. Toss them in French Dressing and leave until cold.

Slice the potatoes into a bowl, add the celery and the mayonnaise and season well. Add most of the chopped chives then cover and leave in a cool place until required. Check the seasoning. Sprinkle with the remaining chives and serve.

SALADE NIÇOISE

A colourful, summery salad from Provence. The traditional way to serve it is in a large, deep glass bowl on a bed of lettuce. I prefer it assembled over a large earthenware platter.

SERVES 8

4 LARGE RED TOMATOES

4 HARD-BOILED EGGS

2 LITTLE GEM LETTUCES,
WASHED AND WITH THE
LEAVES SEPARATED

1 CUCUMBER, SLICED

2 PEPPERS, RED AND YELLOW,
CORED, DESEEDED AND CUT INTO
STRIPS LENGTHWAYS

1 BUNCH SPRING ONIONS,
FINELY SLICED

1 SMALL TIN ANCHOVIES,
DRAINED, AND SNIPPED
INTO PIECES

125 G/4 OZ BLACK OLIVES,
PITTED

1 TABLESPOON CAPERS,
OR TO TASTE

FRENCH DRESSING, TO TASTE
(SEE PAGE 91)

3 TABLESPOONS CHOPPED
FRESH HERBS, SUCH AS
CHIVES, PARSLEY, TARRAGON
AND BASIL, TO GARNISH

To peel the tomatoes, place them in a bowl and cover with boiling water for 1 minute. Drain, slip off the skins, and chill.

Peel the eggs and cut them in half and cut the chilled tomatoes into chunks. Place a layer of lettuce on the platter, then layers of cucumber, eggs, tomatoes, peppers and spring onions, lightly seasoning between the layers. Scatter over the anchovies, olives and capers, and drizzle with French Dressing. Sprinkle with the chopped herbs.

VARIATIONS

I prefer the peppers skinned (grill them until the skin turns black, slip off the skins and remove the seeds). Salade Niçoise or Ratatouille (page 88) make delicious fillings for **Pan Bagnat** – a crispy baguette, filled so the delicious juices seep into the bread. (But don't forget to remove the stones from the olives!)

76

Petits Pois
À la Française

If you grow green peas in your own vegetable garden, you will have the best raw materials for this dish. Peas are best newly-picked. If, like most people, you must get your peas from the greengrocer, buy the greenest, freshest ones you can find. If you are condemned to using the frozen variety, omit the caster sugar.

Put the lettuce in a pan and add the remaining ingredients. Cover tightly then simmer for about 20 minutes, or until the peas are tender.

Remove the lettuce and mint and discard, then spoon the peas into a hot serving dish.

VARIATION

Serve the peas with the lettuce and mint, and add 125 g/4 oz streaky bacon, snipped into strips, and fried until crispy.

PREVIOUS PAGES *Asparagus (recipe page 81), with Mayonnaise (recipe page 93) and French Dressing (recipe page 90).*

SERVES 4

½ SMALL LETTUCE, WASHED

500 G/1 LB SHELLED, FRESH PEAS

4 SPRING ONIONS, SLICED

A FEW SPRIGS OF MINT

2 TABLESPOONS WATER

50 G/2 OZ BUTTER

1 TEASPOON CASTER SUGAR

CORN ON THE COB

Remove the leaves and silk from the corn cobs and wash the cobs thoroughly in cold water. Place in a large pan of boiling water, cover and simmer for about 15 minutes or until tender.

Warm all the ingredients for the lemon butter in a small pan. Drain the corn cobs, toss in a little of the lemon butter. Place them on a serving dish and serve with the remaining lemon butter in a small sauce boat.

SPINACH GRATIN

Young spinach leaves are delicious in salads, especially when combined with crispy bacon and lightly toasted pine nuts. I think spinach is one of the most delicious vegetables, and this Spinach Gratin is a good way to use ordinary spinach, especially if you grow it yourself and have masses of it.

Butter or oil a gratin dish. Remove the stems from the spinach and season with salt and pepper. Lay the spinach leaves in the dish, and press them down. Sprinkle over the breadcrumbs, and drizzle with olive oil. Cook in a preheated oven at 180°C (350°F) Gas Mark 4 for about 1 hour, or until the spinach has wilted down, and the top is browned.

SERVES 6

6 CORN COBS

For the lemon butter
125 G/4 OZ SALTED BUTTER
FRESHLY GROUND BLACK PEPPER
2 TABLESPOONS LEMON JUICE

SERVES 4

1 KG (2 LB) FRESH LEAF
SPINACH, WASHED AND
PATTED DRY

50 G/2 OZ WHITE
BREADCRUMBS

100 ML/3½ FL OZ
EXTRA-VIRGIN OLIVE OIL,
OR TO TASTE

SALT AND FRESHLY GROUND
BLACK PEPPER

CHAMPIGNONS À LA CRÈME

SERVES 4

4 RASHERS BACON

3 LARGE SLICES WHITE BREAD,
CRUSTS REMOVED

3 TABLESPOONS SUNFLOWER OIL

4 TABLESPOONS WHITE WINE

JUICE OF ½ LEMON

500 G/1 LB BUTTON
MUSHROOMS OR SMALL
CHESTNUT MUSHROOMS

150 ML/¼ PINT DOUBLE CREAM

SALT AND FRESHLY GROUND
BLACK PEPPER

Grill the bacon rashers until brown and crisp. Drain on kitchen paper, set aside and keep warm.

Cut the bread into 5mm/¼ inch dice, fry in the oil until golden brown, then drain on kitchen paper.

Pour the white wine and lemon juice into the pan, bring to the boil, add the mushrooms, reduce the heat, and poach for 2 minutes. Lift out with a slotted spoon and drain thoroughly.

Boil the white wine and lemon juice for a few minutes until reduced to about 3 tablespoons. Add the double cream, bring to the boil, add the mushrooms, season and serve with the croûtons and crispy bacon.

CREAMY MUSHROOM SAUCE

SERVES 4

1 ONION, SLICED

25 G/1 OZ BUTTER

500 G/1 LB WHITE OR
CHESTNUT MUSHROOMS,
SLICED

125 ML/4 FL OZ
CRÈME FRAÎCHE

A suitable accompaniment for sautéed pork, veal or chicken, and delicious with grilled meat.

Melt the butter in a small frying pan, and gently fry the onion until coloured but not browned. Add the sliced mushrooms and sauté until tender.

Swirl in the crème fraîche, reduce for a few moments, Season to taste, and serve.

500 G/1 LB COURGETTES

For the batter

125 G/4 OZ PLAIN FLOUR

2 EGGS, SEPARATED

ABOUT 150 ML/¼ PINT MILK

OIL FOR DEEP FRYING

SALT

COURGETTE FRITTERS

Serve as a starter with a tomato coulis, or as a vegetable.

Cut the courgettes in 5 mm/¼ inch slices. Put the flour and salt in a bowl and blend in the egg yolks. Add sufficient milk to make a coating batter. Whisk the egg whites stiffly and fold into the batter.

Heat the oil in a deep fryer or saucepan, dip the sliced courgettes in the batter, then fry until golden brown. Drain on kitchen paper and serve hot.

VARIATIONS

Aubergine Fritters: slice small aubergines diagonally, sprinkle with salt and let stand for 30 minutes. Rinse with cold water, drain and dry. Dip in batter and proceed as before.

Mushroom Beignets: substitute medium-sized mushrooms. Leave whole, dip in batter and proceed as before.

Courgette Flowers: no preparation required. Just dip in batter and fry in oil.

Pepper Fritters: cut strips of red and yellow peppers, dip and fry in oil, as above.

ASPARAGUS

Trim off the white and brown jagged ends of the asparagus and cut all the stalks to equal length. Scrape off the rough skin near the cut end with a sharp knife or vegetable peeler. Wash well in cold water.

Bring a large, shallow pan of salted water to the boil, add the asparagus, cover, and simmer for 7-10 minutes according to thickness, or until just tender. Lift out the asparagus carefully and drain.

Serve hot with Hollandaise Sauce (see page 93) or melted butter, or cold with French Dressing (see page 91).

SERVES 4

500 G/1 LB BUNDLE OF FRESH
ASPARAGUS

SALT

Illustrated page 74-75

LEEKS AU GRATIN

Trim the roots and most of the green part from the leeks. Wash very thoroughly, then cook in boiling salted water for about 10 minutes or until just tender. Drain and arrange in a shallow 1.2 litre/2 pint ovenproof dish, reserving about 4 tablespoons cooking liquid.

Make a roux with the butter and flour, blend in the milk and reserved cooking liquid. Bring to boiling point, stirring. Add most of the cheese, season well with salt and freshly ground black pepper, then add the cayenne pepper. Pour the sauce over the leeks and sprinkle with the remaining cheese. Cook under a medium grill for about 5 minutes.

SERVES 4

4 LEEKS

25 G/1 OZ BUTTER

25 G/1 OZ PLAIN FLOUR

300 ML/½ PINT MILK

75 G/3 OZ GRATED EMMENTAL
CHEESE

25 G/1 OZ GRATED PARMESAN
CHEESE

A PINCH OF CAYENNE PEPPER

SALT AND FRESHLY GROUND
BLACK PEPPER

750 G/1½ LB CHICORY

25 G/1 OZ BUTTER

3 TABLESPOONS WATER

1 TEASPOON LEMON JUICE

1 TEASPOON CASTER SUGAR

SALT AND FRESHLY GROUND
BLACK PEPPER

BRAISED CHICORY

*In France chicory is called 'endive' and endive is called
'chicorie' – all very muddling. Chicory is often thought to be rather
bitter when cooked. I find it best to braise it, adding a little sugar. Do
not, however, leave chicory to soak in water when washing and
trimming, because this will increase the bitterness.*

Place the chicory in a pan of boiling water and boil for about
2 minutes. drain in a colander and rinse with cold water.
Butter a 1.2 litre/2 pint shallow ovenproof dish with half the
butter. Arrange the chicory in the dish. Add the remaining
ingredients, dot with the remaining butter and cover with a
lid. Cook in a preheated oven at 150°C (300°F) Gas Mark 2 for
about 1-1¼ hours until tender.

Lift the chicory carefully from the dish and serve with the
buttery cooking juices.

VARIATION

Chicory à la Mornay: braise the chicory as in the main recipe,
then remove from the dish and pour the cooking juices into a
separate pan. Add 300 ml/½ pint of Mornay Sauce (see page
25) to the juices, and pour a layer of sauce back into the dish.
Lay the chicory over the sauce and spoon over the remainder
of the sauce. Sprinkle with grated Gruyère cheese, dot with
butter and brown in a very hot oven, preheated to 240°C,
475°F, Gas Mark 9.

BAKED FENNEL WITH RED PEPPERS AND PARMESAN

Fennel is often used in summery salads – its juicy, mild, aniseed flavour giving an extra dimension to leafy salads. It is also splendid added to a Salade Niçoise (see page 76).

(see page 76)

SERVES 6

3 HEADS FENNEL

½ RED PEPPER, CUT INTO PENCIL-THIN STRIPS

3-4 TABLESPOONS OLIVE OIL

75 G/3 OZ PARMESAN CHEESE, GRATED

SALT AND FRESHLY GROUND BLACK PEPPER

A LITTLE PAPRIKA PEPPER

Remove the tops from the fennel and cut into 4 wedges. Blanch in boiling salted water for about 10 minutes and drain and refresh in cold water. Toss the blanched fennel and strips of pepper in olive oil until all are coated.

Arrange the fennel in an ovenproof dish, placing strips of pepper in between the quarters of fennel. Season with salt and pepper and sprinkle with grated Parmesan. Dust with paprika.

Bake in a preheated oven at 220°C (425°F) Gas Mark 7 for 15-20 minutes until the fennel is tender. This vegetable dish is a delicious accompaniment for lamb.

VARIATIONS

Braised Fennel: take 3 heads of fennel, sliced into quarters. Heat about 4-5 tablespoons olive oil in a flameproof dish, and gently fry the fennel and 2 finely sliced garlic cloves for about 30 minutes, turning once. Season with salt and freshly ground black pepper, sprinkle with 150 ml/¼ pint white wine and bring to the boil on top of the stove. Dot with butter and cook in the oven as in the main recipe.

Fennel à la Mornay is cooked in the same way as Chicory à la Mornay, described on page 82, opposite.

SERVES 4-6

500 G/1 LB POTATOES, PEELED
AND THINLY SLICED

1 LARGE ONION, THINLY SLICED

50 G/2 OZ BUTTER

SALT AND FRESHLY GROUND
BLACK PEPPER

1 TABLESPOON CHOPPED FRESH
PARSLEY, TO GARNISH

LYONNAISE POTATOES

'A la Lyonnaise' means that a dish – meat, poultry, or vegetables – is prepared using sautéed onions. This is a very good version, baked in the oven.

Blanch the potatoes in boiling water for 1 minute, then drain. Fry the onion in butter for a few minutes, without colouring.

Layer the onion, potatoes and seasoning into a buttered 1.2 litre/2 pint shallow casserole, finishing with a layer of the potatoes. Pour over any butter left in the pan, cover and bake at 200°C (400°F) Gas Mark 6 for 1½ hours. Remove the lid for the last 30 minutes to allow the potatoes to brown. Sprinkle with the chopped fresh parsley, and serve.

SERVES 4-6

500 G/1 LB POTATOES, PEELED

3 TABLESPOONS OLIVE OIL

3 FAT GARLIC CLOVES, CRUSHED

3 TABLESPOONS CHOPPED
FRESH FLAT LEAF PARSLEY,
TO GARNISH

GARLIC FRIED POTATOES

Cut the potatoes in 1 cm/½ inch dice. Fry gently in oil until golden brown. Add garlic to the pan just before serving and mix well. Sprinkle generously with parsley.

DAUPHINE POTATOES

SERVES 4-6

500 G/1 LB POTATOES, COOKED
AND SIEVED

40 G/1½ OZ BUTTER

For the choux paste

50 G/2 OZ BUTTER

150 ML/5 FL OZ WATER

65 G/2½ OZ PLAIN FLOUR,
SIFTED

2 EGGS, BEATEN

OIL FOR DEEP FRYING

SALT AND FRESHLY GROUND
BLACK PEPPER

Dauphine Potatoes and Potatoes Dauphinois are two quite different dishes. I have included both – because they are both delicious.

To make the choux paste

Measure the butter and water into a small pan. Allow the butter to melt and then bring slowly to the boil. Remove the pan from the heat, add the flour all at once, and beat until the mixture forms a soft ball. Allow to cool slightly, then gradually beat in the eggs, beating well between each addition to give a smooth, shiny paste.

To assemble

Mix the potato and butter together, then beat the choux paste together with the potato mixture. Season well and shape into rounds with 2 greased spoons. Fry in hot oil until golden brown, drain on kitchen paper and sprinkle with salt and freshly ground black pepper before serving.

POTATOES DAUPHINOIS

SERVES 4-6

500 G/1 LB POTATOES, PEELED
AND THINLY SLICED

40 G/½ OZ BUTTER

1 FAT GARLIC CLOVE, CRUSHED

300 ML/½ PINT DOUBLE CREAM

SALT AND FRESHLY GROUND
BLACK PEPPER

Wash the sliced potatoes and pat dry with kitchen paper. Butter an ovenproof dish, scatter with crushed garlic, and fill with layers of potato. Pour over the cream and sprinkle with salt and freshly ground black pepper.

Place in a preheated oven at 200°C (400°F) Gas Mark 6 for 1-1½ hours, or until tender. Increase the heat to 220°C (425°F) Gas Mark 7 to brown the top, then serve.

500 G/1 LB SMALL OR MEDIUM
AUBERGINES

500 G/1 LB SLICED ONIONS

300 ML/½ PINT EXTRA-VIRGIN
OLIVE OIL

3 FAT CLOVES OF GARLIC,
CRUSHED

500 G/1 LB LARGE FIRM RIPE
TOMATOES, SKINNED, DESEEDED
AND THICKLY SLICED

2 TABLESPOONS THYME LEAVES

125 G/4 OZ GRATED PARMESAN
CHEESE

1 TABLESPOON CHOPPED FRESH
PARSLEY

125 G/4 OZ BREADCRUMBS

SALT AND FRESHLY GROUND
BLACK PEPPER

Illustrated opposite

TIAN

This is a traditional Provençal dish redolent of summer. It takes its name from the plate in which it is cooked – square or rectangular, with raised edges, about 5 cm/2 inches deep. Traditionally made of glazed earthenware, any attractive ovenproof serving dish will do. Vary the ingredients according to taste, and what's in season.

Slice the aubergines in half if very small, or diagonally if larger. Sprinkle with salt, leave to stand for 30 minutes, rinse in cold water and pat dry.

Sauté the onions in a little oil until soft and golden. Add two-thirds of the garlic half way through the cooking time. Fry the aubergines for a few minutes until lightly browned.

Place a layer of sautéed onions in the bottom of the dish. Place alternate rows of aubergines and tomatoes at an angle, so that they resemble fish scales. Rub the thyme leaves between your palms to release their scent, and sprinkle generously over the tian. Mix the remaining garlic, the grated Parmesan, chopped parsley and breadcrumbs, and scatter over the top, then drizzle over the remaining olive oil, and season to taste.

Bake in a preheated oven at 200°C (400°F) Gas Mark 6 for 20 minutes until cooked and the top browned.

VARIATIONS

Potato and Onion Tian: place thick slices of par-boiled potato alternately with slices of large red onions, blanched, and slices of skinned tomato. Complete as above.

Tian of Chicken and Aubergines: replace the tomatoes with chicken thighs, floured, and browned in oil first. Use baby aubergines, if available, halved and browned in oil.

SERVES 4-6

2 SMALL AUBERGINES

4 COURGETTES

6 TABLESPOONS OLIVE OIL

2 MEDIUM ONIONS, FINELY
SLICED

2 RED PEPPERS, DESEEDED AND
THINLY SLICED

2 GARLIC CLOVES, CRUSHED

500 G/1 LB TOMATOES,
SKINNED, DESEEDED AND
CHOPPED

SALT AND FRESHLY GROUND
BLACK PEPPER

1 TABLESPOON CHOPPED
FRESH PARSLEY

RATATOUILLE

*Ratatouille is good, hot or cold. Make a large quantity and
serve some of it hot with roast or grilled meat. Refrigerate the rest
and serve as an hors d'oeuvre for a summer lunch in the garden,
scattered with sprigs and flowers of basil. It is also rather
nice as the filling for a rustic-style omelette.*

Cut the unpeeled aubergines and courgettes in 1 cm/½ inch
cubes. Place on sheets of kitchen paper and sprinkle with salt.
Leave to drain for 30 minutes.

Heat the olive oil in a large heavy pan. Add the onions and
cook slowly until softened but not coloured.

Dry the aubergines and courgettes with kitchen paper
then add them to the pan with the red peppers and garlic.
Cover and simmer very gently for about 40 minutes. Stir the
vegetables occasionally so the mixture does not stick. Add the
tomatoes and pepper to taste. Cover and cook for a further
20 minutes. Stir in the parsley and serve hot or cold.

FRENCH BAKED ONIONS

*The onions may be peeled, or unpeeled, and served hot with roast
meat, or cold with a French Dressing (see page 91).*

see page 91

Dot the onions with butter, then season with salt and lots of
freshly ground black pepper. Bake in a preheated oven at
180°C (350°F) Gas Mark 4 for 1 hour, until tender and golden.

BAKED GARLIC

*When cooked long and slowly, garlic loses much of its peppery
flavour and becomes mild and nutty. It is especially good served with
French Roast Chicken (see page 51), or as a first course with a mild
goat's cheese and a salad of mixed green leaves such as rocket and
frisée. To eat, press the soft garlic flesh out of the roasted heads, and
spread a little on each piece of cheese or chicken.*

see page 51

Slice the tops off the heads of garlic, to expose the juicy heart
of each clove. Leave the papery shells intact.

Lightly oil a shallow ovenproof dish, and pack the garlic
heads in tightly, cut-side up. Spoon olive oil on to each head,
so the oil seeps between the cloves. Season with salt and freshly
ground black pepper. Bake in a preheated oven at 200°C
(400°F) Gas Mark 6 for about 1 hour, or until very tender.
Spoon over more olive oil occasionally.

To eat, press the soft purée out of the papery shells and
spread over meat, cheese or toast.

SERVES 4

8 LARGE ONIONS, PEELED

50 G/2 OZ BUTTER

SALT AND FRESHLY GROUND
BLACK PEPPER

PER SERVING

1 WHOLE HEAD OF GARLIC
PER PERSON

1 TABLESPOON
EXTRA-VIRGIN OLIVE OIL
PER HEAD OF GARLIC

SALT AND FRESHLY GROUND
BLACK PEPPER

Illustrated page 50

For the infused milk

600 ML/1 PINT MILK

1 ONION, SLICED

1 CARROT, CUT INTO
MATCHSTICKS

6 PEPPERCORNS

1 BAY LEAF

3 PARSLEY STALKS

For a pouring sauce

A GENEROUS
40 G/1½ OZ BUTTER

40 G/1½ OZ PLAIN FLOUR

SALT AND PEPPER

For a coating sauce

2 OZ BUTTER

2 OZ PLAIN FLOUR

SALT AND PEPPER

MAKES 600 ML/1 PINT

25 G/1 OZ BUTTER

1 ONION, SLICED

1 CARROT, SLICED

300 ML/½ PINT WATER

1 TABLESPOON TOMATO PURÉE

300 ML/½ PINT BEEF STOCK

2 SPRIGS PARSLEY

1 SPRIG THYME

1 BAY LEAF

1 TABLESPOON PLAIN FLOUR

1 TABLESPOON REDCURRANT
JELLY

6 TABLESPOONS MADEIRA

BÉCHAMEL SAUCE

*Béchamel is the French version of our white sauce, named after
a famous gourmet of the 17th Century, Louis de Béchameil, Marquis
of Nointel. It is always quicker and easier to make this sauce
with hot milk rather than cold.*

To make infused milk, place the milk, sliced onion, carrot, peppercorns and herbs in a saucepan and bring gently to the boil. Remove from the heat and discard the flavourings before making the sauce.

To make the sauce, gently melt the butter in a saucepan, stir in the flour and cook for 1 minute. Pour the hot infused milk gradually onto the roux, stirring well with a wire whisk to prevent lumps forming.

Cook until the sauce reaches the desired consistency, and season to taste.

MADEIRA SAUCE

*An excellent accompaniment for steak or chops, made with the great
fortified wine from the island of Madeira.*

Melt the butter in a pan, add the vegetables and cook slowly until soft. Add the water, tomato purée, stock and herbs and simmer for 20 minutes. Mix the flour with 2 tablespoons of cold water, add to the sauce, and simmer until thickened.

Stir in the redcurrant jelly and simmer until dissolved. Strain the sauce into a clean pan and stir in the Madeira. Reheat before serving.

FRENCH DRESSING

The traditional ingredients for French Dressing or Vinaigrette are plain olive oil and vinegar with or without lemon juice, used to dress a plain green salad of lettuce leaves. There are now many different flavoured olive oils, nut oils and vinegars, and these will produce dressings which suit different salad ingredients. There are also some French cooks who swear that a salad isn't a salad unless it contains cheese. In France, the sugar in this recipe is omitted, but in our house, we treble this amount of sugar.

Blend the first 6 ingredients together in a bowl. Mix in the oil slowly with a whisk or spoon. Finally, stir in the vinegar or the mixture of vinegar and lemon juice. Taste and adjust the seasoning if necessary.

For a simpler French Dressing that will keep longer, omit the chives or onion and lemon juice. Place all the ingredients into a screw top jar, replace the lid and shake vigorously until well blended. In this way, you can increase the ingredients proportionately, and make a larger quantity at one time. The dressing can be kept in the jar in a cool place for up to 6 weeks.

MAKES ABOUT
250 ML / 8 FL OZ

1 FAT GARLIC CLOVE, CRUSHED

1 TEASPOON DIJON MUSTARD

1 TEASPOON VERY FINELY CHOPPED ONION, OR A FEW FINELY SNIPPED CHIVES

1 TEASPOON CASTER SUGAR

SALT AND FRESHLY GROUND BLACK PEPPER

150 ML / ¼ PINT EXTRA VIRGIN OLIVE OIL

75 ML / ⅛ PINT WHITE WINE VINEGAR OR CIDER VINEGAR, OR HALF EACH OF VINEGAR AND LEMON JUICE

Illustrated page 74-75

SERVES 4-6

3 TABLESPOONS WHITE WINE
VINEGAR

1 TABLESPOON WATER

5 EGG YOLKS

225 G/8 OZ UNSALTED BUTTER

SALT AND FRESHLY GROUND
BLACK PEPPER

HOLLANDAISE SAUCE

*Quick and easy when made in the processor. Instead of
reduced vinegar, you can use lemon juice to flavour the sauce
if you prefer. The best way of keeping Hollandaise warm is to
transfer it to a small, wide-necked vacuum
flask until needed.*

Combine the vinegar, water and seasoning in a small pan,
bring to the boil and reduce until about 1 tablespoon remains.
Fill the processor bowl with boiling water to heat the bowl and
blade, then throw the water away. Process the egg yolks until
really smooth. Melt the butter until just boiling.

With the machine running, add the reduced vinegar and
then the hot butter in a steady flow through the funnel. The
sauce should look like thick mayonnaise. Should it not be as
thick as you would like, heat gently in a heatproof bowl over a
pan of simmering water, whisking until thicker. Taste and
adjust the seasoning as required.

MAYONNAISE

This foolproof method makes a very good mayonnaise. Using whole eggs, it is less rich than one made just from yolks. If you like, replace half the sunflower oil with olive oil. For a thinner mayonnaise, add a little water or milk through the funnel with the motor running.

MAKES 900 ML/1½ PINTS

2 EGGS AT ROOM TEMPERATURE

1 TABLESPOON WINE VINEGAR

1 TEASPOON CASTER SUGAR

1 TEASPOON DRY MUSTARD

SALT AND FRESHLY GROUND
BLACK PEPPER

900 ML/1½ PINTS SUNFLOWER
OIL, OR HALF-AND-HALF OLIVE
AND SUNFLOWER OIL

JUICE OF 1 LARGE LEMON

Illustrated page 74-75

Put all the ingredients except the oil and lemon juice into the processor bowl and process briefly to blend. With the machine running, add the oil through the funnel in a slow, steady stream until it has all been incorporated and the mixture is very thick. Switch on again and add all the lemon juice. Taste and check seasoning.

Serve immediately, or turn out into jars. This mayonnaise will keep for up to a month in the refrigerator.

VARIATIONS

Aïoli: this is the classic French garlic mayonnaise. Add 2 (or more if you like) crushed cloves of garlic to the processor with the first set of ingredients. Add 900 ml/1½ pints good olive oil and complete. Add the lemon juice at the end.

Watercress Mayonnaise: wash and roughly chop a bunch of watercress. process briefly and stir into 300 ml/½ pint of the made mayonnaise. Check seasoning.

Avocado Mayonnaise: roughly chop the flesh of an avocado, put it in the processor bowl with a tablespoon of lemon juice and process briefly. Add 300 ml/½ pint of made mayonnaise and process very briefly to mix. Check seasoning.

Tartare Sauce: put a rounded dessertspoon each of chopped gherkins and capers and a few sprigs of parsley in the bowl of the processor, and process briefly to mix.

Home Pâtisserie

CAKES AND PASTRIES

No book on French cooking would be

complete without a section on cakes and

pastries, those mouth-watering delicacies

which adorn the windows of patisseries

throughout the country.

MAKES ABOUT 30

150 G/5 OZ BUTTER
3 EGGS

150 G/5 OZ CASTER SUGAR

150 G/5 OZ SELF-RAISING FLOUR

GRATED RIND OF 1 LEMON

Illustrated on pages 94-95

MADELEINES

Perhaps the most famous of all French cakes, thanks to the great writer Marcel Proust. These classic shell-shaped sponges are good served on their own with coffee, or with mousses or fruit salad. You do need special tins, available from specialist kitchen shops. It is worth greasing and flouring the tins thoroughly, so the madeleines come out cleanly.

Lightly grease a madeleine tin, dust it with flour and shake off any excess.

Melt the butter in a small pan, taking care not to let it get too hot, then allow to cool slightly. Measure the eggs and caster sugar into a large bowl and whisk until pale and thick. Sift in half the flour and fold in gently with the lemon rind. Pour in half the melted butter around the edge of the bowl and fold in. Repeat using the remaining flour and butter.

Spoon the mixture into the prepared tins so that it is just about level with the tops of the tins.

Bake in a preheated oven at 220°C (425°F) Gas Mark 7, for about 8-10 minutes, until well risen, golden and springy to the touch. Ease out of the tins with a small palette knife and cool on a wire rack. Re-grease and flour the tins, and repeat until all the mixture has been used.

PREVIOUS PAGES
On right, Dark Chocolate Gâteau (recipe page 100); front, Madeleines (recipe this page); rear, Florentines (recipe page 97).

FLORENTINES

*Using non-stick baking paper makes it so much simpler
to get the biscuits off the baking trays. You can simply use a
well-greased baking tray, but be careful not to leave the Florentines
for too long or they will harden before you have a chance to
lift them off. These are very luxurious biscuits, but you
will need patience and accurate scales
to make them.*

MAKES ABOUT 20

50 G/2 OZ BUTTER

50 G/2 OZ DEMERARA SUGAR

50 G/2 OZ GOLDEN SYRUP

50 G/2 OZ PLAIN FLOUR

4 GLACÉ CHERRIES, FINELY
CHOPPED

50 G/2 OZ CANDIED PEEL,
FINELY CHOPPED

50 G/2 OZ MIXED ALMONDS AND
WALNUTS, FINELY CHOPPED

175 G/6 OZ PLAIN CHOCOLATE,
BROKEN INTO PIECES

Illustrated on pages 94-95

Line three baking trays with non-stick baking parchment. Measure the butter, sugar and golden syrup into a small pan and heat gently until the butter has melted. Take the pan off the heat, add the flour, chopped glacé cherries, candied peel and nuts, and stir well to mix.

Spoon teaspoonfuls of the mixture on to the prepared baking trays, leaving plenty of room for them to spread. Bake in a preheated oven at 180°C (350°F) Gas Mark 4, for about 8-10 minutes or until golden brown.

Allow the Florentines to cool on the baking paper before lifting them on to a cooling rack with a palette knife. (If the Florentines have been baked on greased baking trays, then allow them to harden for a few moments, before lifting on to cooling racks to cool completely. If they do become too hard to remove, then pop them back into the oven for a few moments to allow them to soften a little.)

Melt the chocolate in a bowl placed over a pan of hot water. Spread a little melted chocolate over the flat base of each Florentine, mark a zig-zag in the chocolate with a fork and leave to set, chocolate side up, on the cooling rack. Store in an airtight container.

SERVES ABOUT 8

3 EGGS

100 G/4 OZ CASTER SUGAR

75 G/3 OZ SELF-RAISING FLOUR

*For the coffee and brandy
butter cream*

75 G/3 OZ CASTER SUGAR

5 TABLESPOONS WATER

2 EGG YOLKS

175 G/6 OZ BUTTER, SOFTENED

1-2 TABLESPOONS COFFEE
ESSENCE

4 TABLESPOONS BRANDY

To finish

175 G/6 OZ FLAKED ALMONDS,
TOASTED

ICING SUGAR FOR DUSTING

Illustrated opposite

COFFEE AND BRANDY CAKE

Rather boozy, but why not!

Grease and line the base of a 23 cm/9 inch round, deep cake tin with greased greaseproof paper.

Measure the eggs and sugar into a large bowl and whisk at full speed with an electric whisk until the mixture is pale in colour and thick enough to leave a trail when the whisk is lifted. Sift the flour over the surface of the mixture and gently fold in with a metal spoon or spatula.

Turn into the prepared tin and bake in a preheated oven at 190°C (375°F) Gas Mark 5, for 30 minutes until well risen and golden brown. Turn out and leave to cool on a wire rack.

To make the coffee and brandy butter cream

Measure the sugar and water into a heavy-based saucepan. Heat very gently until the sugar has dissolved. Boil steadily for 2-3 minutes, until a temperature of 107°C (225°F) on a sugar thermometer is reached, or until the syrup forms a slim thread when pulled apart between two teaspoons. Place the egg yolks in a bowl and give them a quick stir to break them up. Pour the syrup in a thin stream on to the egg yolks, whisking all the time. Continue to whisk until the butter cream mixture is very soft. Stir in the coffee essence and brandy to flavour.

To assemble

Cut the cake in half horizontally and sandwich with a thin layer of the coffee and brandy butter cream. Spread butter cream over the top and sides of the cake, and then press the toasted almonds all over the cake. Dredge lightly with icing sugar and decorate with rosettes of butter cream on each portion, sprinkled with flaked almonds, if liked.

90 G/3½ OZ SELF-RAISING FLOUR

15 G/½ OZ COCOA

125 G/4 OZ PLAIN CHOCOLATE,
BROKEN INTO PIECES

125 G/4 OZ BUTTER

125 G/4 OZ CASTER SUGAR

5 EGGS, SEPARATED

For the filling

4 ROUNDED TABLESPOONS
APRICOT JAM, WARMED

For the icing

175 G/6 OZ ICING SUGAR,
SIFTED15 G/½ OZ COCOA

50 G/2 OZ BUTTER

50 G/2 OZ PLAIN CHOCOLATE

2 TABLESPOONS MILK

1 TABLESPOON ICING SUGAR
FOR DUSTING (OPTIONAL)

Illustrated on pages 94-95

DARK CHOCOLATE GÂTEAU

Line a 20 cm/8 inch cake tin with greased greaseproof paper.

Sift together the flour and cocoa. Melt the chocolate in a small bowl over a pan of simmering water, remove from the heat and then cool.

Beat the butter and sugar together until pale and creamy. Beat in the egg yolks one at a time, beating them well after each addition. Fold in the flour mixture alternately with the melted chocolate. Whisk the egg whites until they form soft peaks, fold into the cake mixture.

Turn into the prepared tin, and bake in a preheated oven at 180°C (350°F) Gas Mark 4 for about 50 minutes or until a skewer inserted in the centre comes out clean. Turn the cake out on a wire rack to cool. Cut into three layers when cold.

Spread the cut surfaces of the cake with half the apricot jam. Reassemble on the wire rack. Brush the top and sides of the cake with the remaining jam.

To make the icing, sift together the icing sugar and cocoa. Heat the remaining ingredients together gently in a pan until the butter and chocolate have melted. Remove from the heat, add the sifted ingredients and beat until thick. Spread the icing quickly over the cake and leave in a cool place to set. Lightly dust with icing sugar, if liked.

BRIOCHES

Best served warm, and if there happen to be any left, they make an excellent breakfast with butter and marmalade. Use easy-blend dried yeast – you simply stir it into the flour – there's no mixing with water and sugar and waiting for it to go frothy.

MAKES ABOUT 12

250 G/9 OZ STRONG PLAIN
WHITE FLOUR

25 G/1 OZ CASTER SUGAR

50 G/2 OZ BUTTER, CUT INTO
PIECES

15 G/½ OZ EASY-BLEND DRIED
YEAST

ABOUT 3 TABLESPOONS TEPID
MILK

2 EGGS, BEATEN

A LITTLE BEATEN EGG, TO GLAZE

Measure the flour and sugar into a large mixing bowl and rub in the butter until the mixture resembles fine breadcrumbs. Stir in the yeast until thoroughly blended, then add the milk and eggs and work together to form a soft dough.

Knead until smooth in the bowl, then turn out on to a lightly floured surface and knead for at least 5 minutes. This kneading can be done in a food processor and will take just 60 seconds. Return the dough to the bowl, cover with clingfilm and leave in a warm place for about 1 hour, until the dough has doubled in size. Lightly grease 12 fluted brioche moulds or deep fluted patty tins.

Knead the dough again on a floured surface, then divide into 12 equal pieces. Cut off one-quarter from each piece, then form the larger part into a ball and place in the greased tins. Firmly press a hole in the centre of each ball and place the remaining small piece of dough, rolled into a ball, on top of this hole. It should look like a topknot.

Cover all the brioches with clingfilm and leave to prove for another 45 minutes, until light and puffy.

To bake the brioches, glaze with a little beaten egg and bake in a preheated oven at 230°C (450°F) Gas Mark 8, for 10-12 minutes, until golden brown. Gently lift out of the moulds and allow to cool on a wire rack. Serve the brioches warm with butter balls for a special occasion.

Sweet Confections

AND FRUIT AND CHEESE

Most French families finish their meals with fresh fruit and cheese, but even when special desserts are served the dish is usually fairly light. French school children visiting Britain go overboard for roly-poly and suet pudding, but this is because they have no equivalent at home. In this chapter, I have concentrated on delicate, rich dishes which the French do so well.

LES FROMAGES ET LES FRUITS

In France, cheese is served before the pudding – and cheese is certainly better suited to the bigger wines, served with the preceding main course. Serve it as you like – before the pudding, in the French way, or after, in the British way. Or serve it together with a selection of fruit at the end of a summer lunch.

A SELECTION OF FRENCH CHEESES

A SELECTION OF FRUITS IN SEASON

RADISHES

OLIVES

VINE LEAVES OR BLACKCURRANT LEAVES, TO SERVE

Illustrated pages 102-3

Serve a selection of French cheeses such as the ones shown on pages 102 and 103. Clockwise, from left, are; Camembert, Carré de l'Est, Tourée de l'Aubier, Roquefort, Bouignette, Crottin de Chavignon and, in the centre, Fromage de Chèvre Cabris.

Add radishes, olives, and fruit in season, such as fresh figs, cherries, bunches of different coloured grapes and pears. They look beautiful arranged on a big platter with vine leaves. If no vine leaves are available, use blackcurrant leaves.

FRESH FRUIT SALAD

SERVES 8-10

1 LARGE PINEAPPLE

1 MELON, SUCH AS GALIA, OGEN OR CANTELOUPE

2 DESSERT APPLES, CORED AND SLICED

2 PEARS, PEELED, CORED AND SLICED

2 ORANGES, PEELED AND SLICED

1 GRAPEFRUIT, PEELED, WITH SKINS AND SEEDS REMOVED FROM THE SEGMENTS

CASTER SUGAR

1 TABLESPOON COINTREAU

125 G/4 OZ RASPBERRIES OR STRAWBERRIES

Cut the top and leaves (if any) from the pineapple and scoop out the flesh, leaving a wall about 5 mm ¼ inch thick. Discard the core and cut the flesh in small pieces, reserving any juice.

Cut the flesh of the melon into 2.5 cm/1 inch dice.

Put the pineapple and its juice into a bowl with the slices of apple, pear and orange. Add the grapefruit segments and sprinkle with sugar to taste. Add the liqueur, cover and leave in a cool place until the sugar has dissolved.

Add the raspberries or strawberries, stand the pineapple upright and pile the fruit into it. Alternatively, it can be served in an attractive glass bowl.

CRÈME CARAMEL

SERVES 4-6

Do not worry if the custard takes longer to cook than the time given – it will set eventually. Do not increase the oven temperature or the custard will boil and curdle and have an unpleasant texture when finished. If you have some, use vanilla sugar instead of caster sugar and vanilla essence.

To make the caramel

Put the sugar and the water in a heavy pan over a very low heat. Allow the sugar to dissolve slowly without boiling. Bring the syrup to the boil and keep boiling until pale golden brown, then pour quickly into the base of a 900 ml/1½ pint Charlotte mould or cake tin.

To make the custard

Using a fork, blend the eggs, sugar and vanilla essence together in a bowl. Warm the milk in a pan until hand hot, then pour on to the egg mixture, stirring well.

To assemble

Butter the sides of the mould or tin above the caramel. Strain the custard into the mould or tin, and place in a meat tin half filled with hot water (a *bain-marie*, see page 123).

Bake in a preheated oven at 150°C (300°F) Gas Mark 2, for 1½ hours or until a knife inserted in the centre comes out clean. Remove the custard from the oven and leave it to become completely cold, at least 12 hours or overnight, before turning out on to a flat dish just before serving.

For the caramel

75 G/3 OZ CASTER SUGAR

3 TABLESPOONS WATER

For the custard

4 EGGS

40 G/1½ OZ VANILLA SUGAR
(SEE PAGE 9),
OR CASTER SUGAR AND A FEW
DROPS OF VANILLA ESSENCE

600 ML/1 PINT MILK

PREVIOUS PAGES
*Fruit and Cheese, including
(clockwise, from left) Camembert,
Carré de l'Est, Tourée de l'Aubier,
Roquefort, Bouignette, Crottin de
Chavignon and, in the centre,
Fromage de Chèvre Cabris
(recipe page 104).*

SERVES 8

500 G/1 LB CURD CHEESE

200 G/7 OZ FROMAGE FRAIS

2 TABLESPOONS ICING SUGAR,
SIFTED

SALT

Illustrated opposite

COEURS À LA CRÈME

*This classic French dish is elegant and delicious – and
very easy to make. Always serve it well chilled, with extra cream,
accompanied by either fresh strawberries or raspberries.*

Purée the curd cheese in a processor or blender. Beat the fromage frais, icing sugar and salt together until smooth. Blend in the curd cheese.

Turn the mixture into four 175 g/6 oz moulds, preferably heart-shaped, lined with a double thickness of damp muslin. Pack the mixture tightly into the moulds and, from time to time, gently press the liquid out through the muslin. Pour off the liquid from inside the mould whenever it accumulates. Chill overnight in the refrigerator.

Unmould on to a plate, remove the muslin and serve with fresh strawberries or raspberries, sugar and double cream.

3 EGGS, SEPARATED

175 G/6 OZ CASTER SUGAR

600 ML/1 PINT MILK

25 G/1 OZ VANILLA SUGAR
(SEE PAGE 9),
OR CASTER SUGAR AND A FEW
DROPS OF VANILLA ESSENCE

1 HEAPED TEASPOON CORNFLOUR

ILES FLOTTANTES

Serve Floating Islands with red fruit salad or simply on their own. If you have no vanilla sugar, add ½ teaspoon vanilla essence and 25 g/1 oz caster sugar.

Grease a shallow 23 x 25 cm/9 x 10 inch ovenproof dish, in which the Iles Flottantes are to be served.

Whisk the egg whites at full speed in an electric mixer for 1 minute then add the sugar gradually, keeping the whisk at full speed, until the mixture is thick and shiny.

Bring the milk to just below boiling point.

In a separate bowl mix the egg yolks, the vanilla sugar and cornflour and, using a balloon whisk, pour on the hot milk very slowly, whisking all the time.

Return the custard to the heat and cook gently until the froth disappears and the custard is lightly thickened. Pour the custard into the dish and, using two tablespoons, arrange the 10 meringues on top.

Transfer to the oven and bake in a preheated oven at 150°C (300°F) Gas Mark 2, for 15-20 minutes or until the meringues are set and no longer sticky.

ALMOND ICE CREAM

Easy to make and richly flavoured with almonds and caramel.

For the praline

50 G/2 OZ CASTER SUGAR

2 TABLESPOONS WATER

50 G/2 OZ UNBLANCHED ALMONDS

For the ice cream

4 EGGS, SEPARATED

125 G/4 OZ ICING SUGAR

300 ML/½ PINT DOUBLE CREAM, LIGHTLY WHIPPED

Illustrated on page 100, at rear

Slowly heat the caster sugar and water in a pan, until the sugar dissolves. Add the almonds and cook quickly until the mixture is a deep golden brown. Stir frequently.

Turn on to an oiled baking tray. Leave until set, then pulverize in a blender or place the praline between a double layer of greaseproof paper and crush with a rolling pin.

Whisk the egg yolks until blended. In another bowl, whisk the whites until stiff then whisk in the icing sugar, a teaspoon at a time, making a meringue mixture. Whisk the egg yolks into the meringue with the cream. Turn into a plastic container of about 1.5 litre/2½ pint capacity, cover and freeze for 2 hours.

Turn the mixture into a bowl, whisk until smooth, then stir in the praline. Freeze in a covered container until required.

APRICOT ORANGE CREAM

SERVES 6

500 G/1 LB APRICOTS

THINLY PEELED RIND AND JUICE OF 2 LARGE ORANGES

125 G/4 OZ SUGAR

150 ML/¼ PINT WATER

15 G/½ OZ POWDERED GELATINE

300 ML/½ PINT DOUBLE CREAM

½ TEASPOON DEMERARA SUGAR

Stew the apricots and orange rind in the sugar and water, then discard the apricot stones. Purée the apricots, orange rind and syrup in a processor or blender, and stir in the juice of 1 orange.

Put the remaining juice and the gelatine in a small bowl placed over a pan of simmering water. Leave until the gelatine has dissolved, then stir into the apricot mixture and cool.

Whip all but 3 tablespoons of the cream until soft peaks form. When the apricot mixture thickens, fold in the cream.

Pour into a 900 ml/1½ pint glass dish and leave in a cold place until set. Just before serving, pour over the remaining cream and sprinkle with sugar.

PINEAPPLE SORBET

Cut the pineapple in half lengthways, cut out the hard core down the centre of each side. Keep the pineapple shells for serving, if liked. With a grapefruit knife or sharply pointed spoon, scoop out all the flesh and chop finely, saving the juice. Mix the chopped pineapple, juice and lemon juice together. Put the water and sugar in a pan over low heat. Allow the sugar to dissolve slowly, then cool. This makes a thin syrup.

Add the sugar syrup to the pineapple, pour into freezer trays or shallow plastic containers – the total liquid is about 900 ml/1½ pints. Freeze in the freezing compartment of your refrigerator, set to coldest, or in the freezer, until the mixture is set but not hard. Turn the sorbet into a bowl and whisk until broken up and light. Re-freeze, having covered the trays or plastic containers with kitchen foil or lids.

Scoop out the sorbet with a metal spoon that has been dipped in boiling water and serve – in the pineapple shells, if liked, or in individual glass dishes.

SERVES 6

1 MEDIUM-SIZED FRESH
PINEAPPLE

JUICE OF 1½ LEMONS

450 ML/¾ PINT WATER

175 G/6 OZ CASTER SUGAR

Illustrated opposite,
(in foreground)

SORBET AU CASSIS

Bring the water to the boil with the blackcurrants, sugar, grated rind and lemon juice. Reduce the heat and cook very gently until tender. Process to a purée and then strain through a sieve. Stir in the cassis and pour the mixture into a polythene box, let cool, then freeze until it is firm but not quite solid. Process again to break up the ice crystals, then return to the freezer and freeze until solid. Take out of the freezer 10 minutes before serving and serve in small scoops.

SERVES 6

300 ML/½ PINT WATER

500 G/1 LB FRESH
BLACKCURRANTS

250 G/8 OZ GRANULATED SUGAR

GRATED RIND AND JUICE
OF 1 LEMON

4 TABLESPOONS CASSIS
(BLACKCURRANT LIQUEUR)

Illustrated opposite
(centre right)

For the rich shortcrust pastry flan case

375 G / 12 OZ PLAIN FLOUR

1 TABLESPOON ICING SUGAR

200 G / 7 OZ BUTTER

ABOUT 9 TEASPOONS WATER

For the fruit filling

1.5 KG / 3 LB APRICOTS

300 ML / ½ PINT WATER

2 TABLESPOONS SUGAR

For the confectioners' custard

3 EGGS

75 G / 3 OZ VANILLA SUGAR
(SEE PAGE 9),
OR CASTER SUGAR AND A FEW
DROPS OF VANILLA ESSENCE

3 TABLESPOONS PLAIN FLOUR

450 ML / ¾ PINT MILK

For the arrowroot glaze

3 TEASPOONS ARROWROOT

300 ML / ½ PINT FRUIT JUICE

2 TABLESPOONS APRICOT
BRANDY OR COGNAC

APRICOT TART

Equally delicious with poached fresh nectarines, plums or peaches.

To make the pastry

Make the pastry as described on page 26, and use it to line a 28 cm/11 inch shallow, fluted flan tin with a removable base. Line with greaseproof paper and baking beans or foil, and bake 'blind' (see page 122) in a preheated oven at 200°C (400°F) Gas Mark 6, for 25 minutes. Remove the paper and baking beans or foil. Bake for a further 5 minutes to dry the base of the flan case. Remove from the oven and leave to cool.

To make the fruit filling

Halve the apricots and crack the kernels. Place the apricot halves and their kernels in a saucepan with the water and the sugar. Bring to the boil, reduce the heat and poach until tender. Remove the kernels and discard.

To make the confectioners' custard

Blend the eggs with the vanilla sugar or caster sugar and flour. Boil the milk, cool slightly, then add 4 tablespoons of the egg mixture, stir, and slowly stir the milk back into the rest of the mixture, a little at a time. Return to the pan, bring to boiling point, reduce and simmer, stirring, for 2-3 minutes until thick. Remove from the heat and stir frequently so that a skin does not form. Add the vanilla essence if using. Cool.

To assemble

Spread the cold custard in the base of the flan case and arrange the apricots, skin-side up, on top of the custard. Put the arrowroot in a pan, blend in the fruit juice and simmer until thick. Stir in the apricot brandy or cognac. Spoon or brush the glaze over the fruit and leave until set.

Tarte aux Fraises

SERVES 8

For the pastry

250 G/8 OZ SHORTCRUST
PASTRY, MADE WITH
250 G/8 OZ PLAIN FLOUR, ETC.
(SEE PAGE 26)

For the filling

500 G/1 LB STRAWBERRIES,
HULLED

1 TABLESPOON ICING SUGAR

CONFECTIONERS' CUSTARD
(SEE APRICOT TART, PAGE 112)

3 ROUNDED TABLESPOONS
REDCURRANT JELLY

1 TABLESPOON WATER

To make the pastry

Make the pastry as described on page 26, and use it to line a 23 cm/9 inch shallow, fluted flan tin with a removable base. Line with greaseproof paper and baking beans, or with foil, and bake 'blind' (see page 122) in a preheated oven at 200°C (400°F) Gas Mark 6, for 25 minutes. Remove the paper and baking beans or foil. Bake for a further 5 minutes to dry the base of the flan case. Remove from the oven and leave to cool.

To assemble

Cut the strawberries in half, and sprinkle with icing sugar. Place the cooled pastry case on to a flat serving plate. Spread the cold confectioners' custard in the flan case. Cover with the strawberries, cut side downwards.

Put the redcurrant jelly and water in a small pan, and simmer for 2 minutes, then brush over the strawberries to give a shiny finish. Set aside to cool completely.

For the pâté sucrée

100 G/4 OZ PLAIN FLOUR

50 G/2 OZ BUTTER, SOFTENED

50 G/2 OZ CASTER SUGAR

2 EGG YOLKS

For the frangipane

50 G/2 OZ BUTTER, SOFTENED

50 G/2 OZ CASTER SUGAR

1 EGG, BEATEN

50 G/2 OZ GROUND ALMONDS

15 G/½ OZ PLAIN FLOUR

A FEW DROPS OF ALMOND ESSENCE

To finish

50 G/2 OZ FLAKED ALMONDS

ABOUT 3 TABLESPOONS OF APRICOT JAM

FRANGIPANE TARTS

Pâté sucrée is the classic French sweet pastry. I make mine in the food processor, or in a bowl, which is easier than the traditional way.

To make the pâté sucrée

Measure the flour into a bowl or food processor. If making by hand, rub the butter into the flour with the fingertips, until the mixture resembles fine breadcrumbs. Stir in the sugar, then add the egg yolks and mix until the ingredients come together to form a dough. Knead the mixture gently until smooth. (If making in the food processor, process the flour, butter and sugar briefly, add the egg yolks and process until just blended.) Wrap up the dough in clingfilm and leave it to rest in the refrigerator for about 30 minutes.

Roll out the pastry on a lightly floured work surface. Cut out 12 rounds using a 7.5 cm/3 inch plain pastry cutter. Re-roll the trimmings once only. Ease the pastry rounds into the patty tins, and prick lightly with a fork. Chill.

To make the frangipane

Measure the butter and sugar into a bowl and beat well until light and fluffy. Gradually beat in the egg, then stir in the ground almonds, flour and almond essence.

To assemble

Fill the chilled tartlet cases with the frangipane and scatter the flaked almonds on top. Bake in a preheated oven at 190°C (375°F) Gas Mark 5, for about 15 minutes until the frangipane is golden and firm to the touch. Ease the tartlets out of the tin and on to a wire rack.

Sieve the apricot jam into a small pan and warm gently. Brush the tartlets with the apricot glaze, and leave to cool.

TARTE AUX POIRES

A very rich and delicious tart, usually made with apples, though we like it with pears, or with brandy-soaked prunes in Tarte aux Pruneaux

SERVES 8

3 SMALL PEARS

4 TABLESPOONS APRICOT JAM

1 TABLESPOON LEMON JUICE

For the rich shortcrust pastry

250 G/8 OZ SHORTCRUST PASTRY, MADE WITH 250 G/8 OZ PLAIN FLOUR, ETC. (SEE PAGE 26)

For the frangipane

125 G/4 OZ BUTTER, SOFTENED

125 G/4 OZ CASTER SUGAR

2 EGGS, BEATEN

125 G/4 OZ GROUND ALMONDS

50 G/2 OZ PLAIN FLOUR

A FEW DROPS OF ALMOND ESSENCE

1 TABLESPOON SINGLE CREAM

1 TABLESPOON CALVADOS, POIRE WILLIAM, OR OTHER PEAR BRANDY (OPTIONAL)

For the glaze

1 TABLESPOON APRICOT JAM, SIEVED

1 TABLESPOON LEMON JUICE

To make the pastry

Make the pastry as described on page 26, and use it to line a 23 cm/9 inch shallow, fluted flan tin with a removable base. Line with greaseproof paper and baking beans, or with foil, and bake 'blind' (see page 122), in a preheated oven at 200°C (400°F) Gas Mark 6 for 25 minutes. Remove the paper and baking beans or foil, and bake for a further 5 minutes to dry the base of the flan case. Remove from the oven and cool.

To make the frangipane

Beat the butter and sugar until light and fluffy. Gradually beat in the egg, the ground almonds, flour, almond essence, cream and Calvados or pear brandy, if using.

To assemble

Spread the frangipane over the base of the pastry case. Peel, core and halve the pears, place them on a board, cut side down, and slice across thinly. Press them down slightly with the flat of your hand, so the slices overlap. Place the halves in the flan case, rounded side up and press gently into the frangipane.

Melt the jam with the lemon juice, then brush half of it over the pears.

Place in a preheated oven at 200°C (400°F) Gas Mark 6, for 15 minutes, then reduce to 190°C (375°F) Gas Mark 5, and cook for another 20 minutes. Remove from the oven when golden, brush with the remaining melted jam, and bake for another 5-10 minutes. Serve warm.

625-750 G / 1¼-1½ LB BLACK
CHERRIES

2 TABLESPOONS CASTER SUGAR

1 TABLESPOON BRANDY

250 G / 8 OZ PLAIN FLOUR

PINCH OF SALT

3 EGGS, SEPARATED

300 ML / ½ PINT MILK

50 G / 2 OZ CASTER SUGAR

15 G / ½ OZ BUTTER

VANILLA SUGAR, TO SERVE

CLAFOUTIS

This traditional cherry custard is usually made without stoning the cherries. This makes Clafoutis rather fiddly to eat, but if the stones are removed, the final result is too liquid. Use the biggest, firmest cherries you can find, and serve with cream or clotted cream. (Not very French, but delicious!)

Butter a 1.8 litre/3 pint ovenproof dish. Sprinkle the cherries with the 2 tablespoons sugar and the brandy, and set aside for about 30 minutes.

Measure the flour and salt into a bowl. Add the egg yolks and enough milk to make a pouring batter. Whisk the egg whites with the remaining sugar until they form stiff peaks. Fold them into the batter. Pour the batter into the prepared dish and spoon the cherry mixture over. Dot with butter.

Bake in a preheated oven at 190°C (375°F) Gas Mark 5, for about 40 minutes until well risen, firm and golden brown. Serve, dusted with vanilla sugar (see page 9) and a jug of cream – or clotted cream.

TARTE TATIN

Tarte Tatin is the 'upside-down' apple tart, served as a pudding rather than as a cake. In France it is always made with dessert apples, and is best made and eaten on the same day.

To make the pastry

Measure the flour, butter and icing sugar into a bowl and rub in the butter until the mixture resembles fine breadcrumbs. Add the egg yolk and enough water to bring the mixture together to a firm but not sticky dough. Knead lightly, wrap and chill for about 30 minutes.

To make the topping

Measure the butter into a small pan and heat gently until melted. Pour into the base of a 23 cm/9 inch shallow cake tin and sprinkle with the sugar. Peel, core and thinly slice the apples and sprinkle with the lemon juice and rind. Arrange a single layer of the best apples in a circular pattern over the sugar and butter. Cover with the remainder of the apple.

To assemble

Roll out the chilled pastry and use to cover the apples. Bake in a preheated oven at to 200°C (400°F) Gas Mark 6, for about 20 minutes, or until the pastry is crisp and golden-brown. (When cooked, the pastry will have shrunk a little.)

To serve

Tip the juices from the cake tin into a small pan. Turn the tart out on to a plate with the pastry on the bottom. Reduce the juices to a syrupy caramel and pour over the apple. Should there be very little juice – it will depend on the apples – add a couple of tablespoons of demerara sugar, dissolve in a pan with the juices and cook until syrupy.

SERVES ABOUT 6

For the pastry

100 G/4 OZ SELF-RAISING FLOUR

50 G/2 OZ BUTTER, CUBED

1 TABLESPOON ICING SUGAR, SIFTED

1 EGG YOLK

SCANT TABLESPOON COLD WATER

For the topping

75 G/3 OZ BUTTER

75 G/3 OZ DEMERARA SUGAR

900 G/2 LB COX'S OR SIMILAR DESSERT APPLES

FINELY GRATED RIND AND JUICE OF 1 LEMON

For the choux paste

50 G/2 OZ BUTTER

150 ML/5 FL OZ WATER

65 G/2½ OZ PLAIN FLOUR,
SIFTED

2 EGGS, BEATEN

For the filling and icing

300 ML/½ PINT DOUBLE CREAM,
LIGHTLY WHIPPED

250 G/8 OZ ICING SUGAR

1 TABLESPOON COCOA

1 TABLESPOON RUM

1-2 TABLESPOONS WARM WATER

Illustrated opposite

CHOCOLATE PROFITEROLES

Choux pastry is not difficult to make – in fact it's one of the easiest of the pastries. It's important to dry out the little profiteroles once they have become golden in colour.

To make the choux paste

Measure the butter and water into a small pan. Allow the butter to melt and then bring slowly to the boil. Remove the pan from the heat, add the flour all at once, and beat until the mixture forms a soft ball. Allow to cool slightly, then gradually beat in the eggs, beating well between each addition to give a smooth shiny paste.

Place the choux paste mixture into a large piping bag fitted with a 1 cm/½ inch plain nozzle. Pipe 20 blobs of paste on to a greased baking tray.

Bake in a preheated oven at 220°C (425°F) Gas Mark 7, for 10 minutes, then reduce the oven temperature to 190°C (375°F) Gas Mark 5, for a further 15-20 minutes until golden brown. Split one side of each bun so the steam can escape. Set aside to cool on a wire rack.

To assemble

Fill each bun with whipped cream. Sift the icing sugar and cocoa into a bowl. Stir in the rum and sufficient warm water to make a thick glacé icing. Spear each bun with a fork and dip the tops in icing. Pile up in a traditional pyramid as each one is finished, or place in an attractive glass serving bowl. Serve the same day.

For the sweet pastry crust

75 G/3 OZ BUTTER

40 G/1½ OZ CASTER SUGAR

75 G/3 OZ PLAIN FLOUR

40 G/1½ OZ CORNFLOUR

For the choux paste

25 G/1 OZ BUTTER

75 ML/3 FL OZ WATER

30 G/1¼ OZ PLAIN FLOUR

1 EGG, BEATEN

For the pastry cream

3 EGG YOLKS

150 G/5 OZ VANILLA SUGAR
(SEE PAGE 9),
OR CASTER SUGAR AND A FEW
DROPS OF VANILLA ESSENCE

40 G/1½ OZ PLAIN FLOUR

300 ML/½ PINT BOILED MILK

2 EGG WHITES

For the caramel

125 G/4 OZ CASTER SUGAR

2 TABLESPOONS WATER

For the decoration

125 G/4 OZ WHITE GRAPES,
HALVED AND DESEEDED, FROSTED
WITH ICING SUGAR

GÂTEAU ST HONORÉ

*This classic French dessert takes quite a while
to prepare and cook, but it is well worth it for a special occasion.
The result is spectacular!*

To make the pastry

Cream the butter and sugar together. Stir in the flours then roll out to a 20 cm/8 inch circle and place on a baking tray. Bake in a preheated oven at 160°C (325°F) Gas Mark 3, for about 20 minutes or until pale golden brown at the edges. Set aside to cool on a wire rack.

To make the choux paste

Follow the method for making choux paste, and baking the choux puffs, as described on page 118 for Profiteroles.

To make the pastry cream

Blend the egg yolks with 75 g/3 oz of the sugar and the flour. Add the boiled milk gradually and cook over a low heat in the pan until thick. Cool, then add the vanilla essence if using.

Whisk the egg whites until very stiff, and then fold in the remaining sugar. Fold into the yolk mixture. Fill the choux buns with some of the cream.

To assemble

Dissolve the sugar and water for the caramel in a heavy pan. Boil until pale golden then dip the choux buns, on a fork, into the caramel. Quickly arrange the buns around the edge of the pastry base; the caramel will stick them together.

Fill the centre with the remaining cream and pile the white frosted grapes on top.

CRÊPES SUZETTE

For entertaining, prepare the pancakes and the sauce in advance and assemble just before serving, heating the pancakes in the sauce.

To make the crêpes

Make a well in the centre of the flour, add the eggs and half the milk. Whisk until smooth, then gradually add the rest of the milk. Stir in the butter or oil.

Put the oil for frying in a 15-18 cm/6-7 inch heavy-based frying pan and heat slowly. When it is really hot, pour off the excess oil and spoon 2 tablespoons of the batter into the pan. Tip the pan slightly from side to side so that the batter thinly covers the base. Cook the pancake for about 1 minute, then turn it over and cook for another minute. Put the pancake on a plate and cover it with a clean tea towel. Repeat with the remaining batter, stacking the pancakes on top of each other.

To make the sauce

Put the sugar, butter, orange rind and juice into a pan. Heat gently until the sugar has dissolved, then simmer the sauce for about 5-10 minutes until syrupy.

To assemble

Place a pancake in the frying pan, fold it in four, remove from the pan, place on a serving dish and keep it hot. Repeat with the remaining pancakes.

When they have all been coated, add the liqueur and brandy to the pan, and replace the folded pancakes. Reheat the sauce and then serve the pancakes.

Note: to flambé the crêpes, add liqueur to the pan, replace the pancakes and reheat gently. Warm the brandy in a ladle or small saucepan, pour it over the pancakes and set alight.

SERVES 4

For the crêpes

125 G/4 OZ PLAIN FLOUR

2 EGGS

300 ML/½ PINT MILK

1 TABLESPOON MELTED BUTTER OR OIL

1 TABLESPOON OIL FOR FRYING

For the sauce

125 G/4 OZ CASTER SUGAR

125 G/4 OZ BUTTER

GRATED RIND AND JUICE OF 2 ORANGES

1 TABLESPOON OF EITHER CURAÇAO, GRAND MARNIER OR OTHER ORANGE LIQUEUR

3 TABLESPOONS BRANDY

COOKS' NOTES

Both metric and imperial measurements have been given in all recipes. Use one set of measurements only, and not a mixture of both.

Standard level spoon measurements are used in all recipes.
1 tablespoon = one 15 ml spoon   1 teaspoon = one 5 ml spoon

Eggs should be size 3 unless otherwise stated.

Milk should be full fat unless otherwise stated.

Pepper should be freshly ground black pepper unless otherwise stated.

Fresh herbs should be used unless otherwise stated. If unavailable use dried herbs as an alternative, but halve the quantities stated.

To keep parsley and other herbs fresh for longer, place their stems in a jug of water, cover the jug completely with a polythene bag – they will keep fresh for a fortnight in the refrigerator.

A *bouquet garni* is a small bundle of herbs tied together with string. They are removed before serving. It usually consists of 2 or 3 sprigs of parsley, a sprig of thyme, a couple of bay leaves and often a stick of celery. In Provençal recipes, a sprig of rosemary is also included. A *bouquet garni* can also be bought as a selection of dried herbs, tied up in a little muslin bag.

To bake 'blind': to produce a crisp pastry case, the case is often cooked first, before adding a filling. Press the pastry into the flan ring, cover with greaseproof paper, then fill with baking beans, ordinary dried beans or dried pasta. Bake in a preheated oven at the temperature and time indicated, then remove the paper and beans. Return to the oven for a further 5 minutes. Alternatively, the paper and beans may be replaced by a sheet of plain kitchen foil, and filled with crumpled foil.

To cook a dish in a *bain-marie* (e.g. Pâté Maison on page 20), pour the mixture into the casserole or loaf tin. Place the casserole in a roasting tin, and pour cold water into the tin so that the water comes about half way up the sides of the casserole. The sides of the pâté will then cook evenly, where they would otherwise be hard and crusty.

Beurre manié is the traditional French method used to thicken soups and stocks (e.g. Moules Marinière on page 34). Blend 25g/1 oz butter with 25 g/1 oz plain flour until the mixture forms a ball. Pinch off small pieces off the ball of *beurre manié* and stir into the soup or stock until the mixture thickens.

To 'reduce' a stock, remove solids such as meat or vegetables, and boil the liquid hard until a percentage of the water has been boiled off. This increases the flavours and thickens the stock. Reduction sauces are made by boiling the stock even further until a thick, flavourful sauce remains. Take care not to burn the sauce, or boil it dry. Do not add salt to a stock at the beginning of the cooking process, as the resulting stock or sauce may become too salty.

To skin tomatoes, place them in a bowl and pour over boiling water. After 1 minute, pour off the water and slip off the skins. To remove the seeds, scoop them out with a teaspoon. To reduce the water content further, sprinkle the tomatoes with salt, let stand for 10 minutes, and discard the juice.

'Degorging' removes excess water or bitter juices from vegetables such as aubergines, cucumbers and courgettes. To degorge, slice them, then sprinkle generously with salt. Let stand for about 30 minutes, rinse, then pat dry with a clean tea towel or kitchen paper. Degorging removes the bitter juices of aubergines, and excess liquid from any vegetables. The bitter juices may also be removed from aubergines by blanching them in boiling water for a few minutes.

To skin peppers, place them on a carving fork and char over a bare flame, such as a gas ring, or grill them under a hot grill until the skin turns black. Place the charred peppers in a plastic bag for a few minutes, and the skin can be scraped off gently with the back of a knife.

To make Shortcrust Pastry, follow the method on page 27, using the following ingredients:

> 250 g/8 oz flour; 125 g/4 oz butter; 3 tablespoons cold water
> 175 g/6 oz flour; 75 g/3 oz butter; 2 tablespoons cold water
> 125 g/4 oz flour; 50 g/2 oz butter; 1 tablespoon cold water.

It is not advisable to serve raw or partially cooked eggs to people who are very young, very old, ill, or to pregnant women.

INDEX